P9-CET-573

Praise for *You Should Totally Get an MBA*

"Ollinger brings a fresh eye and a comedic perspective to the MBA world."
— *John Byrne, Editor-in-Chief,* **Poets & Quants**

"A hilarious read and pretty damn solid advice for any young professional considering the MBA."
— **Greg Coleman, President, Buzzfeed,**
Adjunct Professor, NYU Stern School of Business

"...delivering relevant career guidance and big laughs in equal measure, Ollinger nails the upper right quadrant on the funny-useful matrix.'"
— *Mitch Galbraith, CEO,* **Funny or Die**

"This book echoes what I've tried to build into my teams throughout my career: our work is serious, but our jobs make up a big part of our lives, so we've got to keep laughing."
— *Geoff Cottrill, Vice Chairman, Grammy Foundation*

"Ollinger has just invented the 'funny-motivational' category of business books."
— *Jesse Itzler, Co-Founder, Marquis Jets,*
Author of **Living With a Seal,** *An owner of the Atlanta Hawks*

"Paul wasn't the smartest guy in our class, but…wait, no actually, that's really all I wanted to say."
— *Helen W. Kurtz, Vice President, General Mills, Inc., Tuck '97*

"I've managed to survive in business without an MBA, but this book makes me wish I had gotten one. (Not really, but Paul asked me to write that.)"
— *Jimmy Pitaro, Media executive*

"Paul's writing is funny and sometimes bizarre, but he knows what he's talking about. If you're thinking about applying to business school, you have to read this book."
— *Kerry Trainor, CEO, Vimeo*

"All the publishers who passed up the opportunity to publish this awesome book are morons."
— *Wenda Harris Millard, President & COO, Medialink*

You Should Totally Get an MBA:
A Comedian's Guide to Top U.S. Business Schools

Copyright © Paul Ollinger 2016. All Rights Reserved.

First published by Absolutely Huge Books
(a subsidiary of Absolutely Huge Company, LLC)
Atlanta, GA

ISBN 13: 978-0-9972706-0-0

Images from *The New Yorker* and *Beavis & Butthead* used with
permission. Jet and Porsche photos from Flickr: https://goo.gl/EJGdgM,
https://goo.gl/f3QYx7
Book design by Adam Robinson for Good Book Developers

www.PaulOllinger.com
Contact info: Media@StandUpSelling.org
Twitter: @Paul_Ollinger
LinkedIn: in/paulollinger

YOU SHOULD **TOTALLY** GET AN MBA

*A Comedian's Guide
to Top U.S. Business Schools*

PAUL OLLINGER

ABSOLUTELY HUGE BOOKS

ATLANTA 2016

HOW TO READ THIS BOOK

Two decades after arriving at Dartmouth's Tuck School of Business I wrote this book with the goal of providing insights to the younger version of me who was considering an MBA.

I had three goals for this project:

- Be useful to the reader.
- Be sincere and objective.
- Don't get sued.

Imparting all the wisdom of the creepy uncle who bought you beer when you were a minor, I cover life's major topics: Work. Relationships. Rogaine.

While this book is obviously a precious work of art and should be regarded as such, don't feel like you have to read it straight through like a novel. For example, Chapter 9 provides background on twenty-five different programs, of which you may only be interested in five.

Just because I took several months of my finite time on this planet to research all of these schools and turn that data into a hilarious and concise portrait of the programs doesn't mean you have to read them all. Hey, what do I care?*

Point being, it's totally fine if you leave this book in your powder room and read it in five minutes increments. I would be honored to be part of your daily ritual.

It is worth noting that this edition covers only U.S. business schools. I chose this focus because the U.S. is the market I know. Yet, in so doing I have foregone discussion of some of the very best schools in the world, like London Business School, Insead, IESE and many others.

So you know what that means? Sequel, baby! Get ready for: *Usted Should Absolument Get an MBA, Deux: Edizione International.* (I'm still fine-tuning the title.)

Not only do I get a tax-deductible trip to China, India and Europe out of it, I'm going to adapt it into a screenplay and pitch it to the Hollywood studios. I envision Selena Gomez playing a tri-lingual, smoky-eyed chanteuse who leaves behind the drudgery of fame to pursue a career in the glamorous world of global strategy consulting.

Want to be my agent?

*Please read them. Please.

CONTENTS

To my parents, whose example was the best education of all.

(Sorry for all the profanity.)

Industry need not wish.

—*Benjamin Franklin*

FOREWORD

By John A. Byrne, Editor-in-Chief of PoetsandQuants.com

I FIRST MET PAUL OLLINGER NEARLY TWO YEARS AGO WHEN he had just started writing the book in your hands. During a long lunch at a small table in downtown San Francisco, I found myself captivated by his life's story and his comedic perspective on MBAs.

Even though he graduated from Dartmouth College's prestigious Tuck School of Business in 1997, and had therefore taken the GMAT 21 years ago, he asked me what I thought about putting himself back in applicant mode and re-taking the challenging exam. I urged him to do so and to write about the experience for us at Poets & Quants. Paul followed through on the crazy pursuit—and I felt drawn to him for the chutzpah he displayed in sitting for the test that nearly every MBA applicant loves to hate and for his witty, irreverent views.

His resulting essay was rip-roaring funny, a vicarious escapade that was both wildly amusing and oddly absurd. My favorite line: "My brain felt like it was in the same shape as my middle-aged body. Which means that my frontal lobe is balding and my cerebellum sports man-boobs and a muffin-top. Perhaps it's natural atrophy, but it couldn't have been helped by 15 years of trans-scalp Rogaine absorption."

That's a clue as to what you'll discover here in the book that is akin to an extended stand-up comic routine. One thing's for sure. You'll find yourself dipping into this treasure of a book for a laugh or two when you most need it (and if you are applying to a school that routinely rejects 75% or more of the people who apply, you are going to need to laugh out loud more frequently than you could ever imagine).

The unmistakable conclusion: Paul Ollinger is one funny guy.

Sure, he's supposed to be funny. After all, he has spent years in stand-up comedy.

But Paul also has had a successful career in the Age of the Internet, having done a startup and worked for four years at Yahoo! and another four at Facebook. And he thinks and writes from the perspective of someone who has been fully indoctrinated into the Master of the Universe culture of MBAs.

This is all another way of saying that given his background, modern-day experience and sometimes sick sense of humor, you would have a hard time finding a better person to author a book on the entire MBA experience and to comment on whether it is worth it. His answer, by the way, is unabashedly in the title: *You Should Totally Get an MBA*.

For anyone about to plunge into what will no doubt become an obsessive quest to get into a highly selective business school, *You Should Totally Get an MBA* is totally a guide you want in your briefcase or knapsack, next to your laptop or on your bedside table. Hell, it could even help you hook up at the local Starbucks if you proudly display it while sipping your Caramel Macchiato.

That's because, as Paul so aptly tells us, young professionals who are thinking about getting an MBA are an impressive and alluring bunch.

Paul's book is a hilarious romp through that often anxiety-filled journey toward an e-mail box filled with ding and admit letters. Time and time again, his musings on everything from GMAT test scores and business school rankings to whether you should get a JD or an MBA are so downright funny that you will immediately find yourself reading them aloud to friends and loved ones. In no time at all, you'll have them laughing along with you.

One of my favorites has to do with his interpretation of scores on the test nearly all business school candidates take, the GMAT.

Get a 700 to a 749, writes Paul, and "You're in the zone. It's no slam-dunk, but you are super-admittable."

What about the poor soul who gets a 500 to 549? "You might be super-nice," advises Paul, "but you're not super-smart. Look on the bright side—the MBA program that finds you to be an attractive candidate will likely have an excellent football team."

Or why not consult his own rankings, which frankly make as much sense as many of the well-known media rankings out there? Paul ranks schools by the average temperature in January as well as their proximity to the nearest Cinnabon.

Aside from the jokes, or in spite of them, you'll find much truth in *You Should Totally Get an MBA*. His humorous observations are almost always on the mark, whether he's hand holding the reader through a tour of the most likely post-MBA jobs from brand management to private equity, or on what to say and not to say during your admissions interview.

Hint: Don't say, "I did, like, SO MANY drugs in college." Do say, "My extensive undergraduate extracurricular activities sometimes interfered with top academic performance."

Paul succinctly dishes on each school's attributes, explores MBA-speak ranging from the 2x2 Matrix to NPV (net present value), and the often peculiar vernacular of the AdCom (admissions committee) folk, from pit-divers, who he defines as "ass-kissing members who chase up to the professor after class," to poets and quants, the latter described as those who are "really great at math but sometimes bad at showering."

But you'll find all this out and so much more by picking up this book and thumbing through it. Quick. You should totally buy this book. You should totally laugh out loud at its often wacky-but-true insights! You should totally get an MBA! Now!

INTRODUCTION

IN 1995 I WAS 25 YEARS OLD, BROKE AS HELL AND SWEATING my ass off in the sticky heat of Memphis, TN. I was working a low-paying job, eating Ramen noodles for dinner and driving a crappy car with no air conditioning.

Suffice to say that I was having very little success in the romance department.

Then one day I got a letter that changed my life. It set me on the course for solid corporate employment in the middle run, affluence in the long run—and amorous success in the short run. In fact, the evening I received said missive, I told a very attractive woman about it. She was so impressed that she consented to make smooshy-face with me in the bar parking lot. (We were in a bar. Did I mention that?)

Twenty years later, I'm financially secure, and have beautiful children and a gorgeous wife. (Winky emoticon.)

You're probably thinking, "Tell me, Paul—what *was* this letter that so impacted your life? Was it your Publishers Clearing House sweepstakes notification?"

No.

"Was it your Herbalife distribution franchise permit?"

No.

"Was it the fashion modeling contract you so richly deserved?"

No. Unfortunately the modeling contract didn't come to fruition. It turns out that Ford Modeling Agency doesn't actually have a "Husky and Balding" division, as I was led to believe by my "model development liaison" at Barbizon.

But even though the letter didn't take me to the world of fashion, it did lead me to the land of The Beautiful People (well, The Semi-Beautiful People anyway).

Before I tell you about the letter, let me ask: would you like to get a letter that changes your life? A letter that sets you on the path to a great career and financial solvency? A letter that leads to parking lot smooshy-face with an attractive smooshy-face partner?

By the way—why am I asking all of these rhetorical questions? Am I trying to be mysterious? Am I trying to heighten tension? Am I trying to get you to sign up for a cult or something?

Well, kind of, yeah.

Because what I'm talking about here is business school, which you should already know from the title of the book (if you didn't know what I was leading up to, then you're not very bright and should stop considering graduate school of any kind).

The letter was my invitation to join the Class of 1997 at Dartmouth's Tuck School of Business. It was a by-product of me getting off my lazy post-college ass and actually doing something to get my career going in the right direction.

The letter represented a yearlong quest to get myself admitted to one of the top MBA programs in the country. It meant that I had hurdled the GMAT, survived the on-campus interview and passed the mental probe of the application essay. It was my golden ticket to the financial chocolate factory, and—as I'm sure you'll agree—chocolate money kicks Ramen's ass.

Of course it wasn't the letter itself that changed my life. It was what the letter represented—the doors that were now open to me. Doors that represented amazing career and life opportunities, should I choose to walk through them with some purpose, punctuality and acceptable personal hygiene.

Now, with almost 20 years and a great career (including stops at Yahoo!, Facebook and the Improv) between business school and today, I find myself reflecting on the business school experience with immense gratitude, and also with a great deal more perspective.

I can see now that I should have had better career direction right out of college and, perhaps, wouldn't have needed business school to focus my energies. But knowing that today is somewhat moot and does little good for the 25-year-old me who could barely afford to get the Ramen stains dry-cleaned out of his TJ Maxx neckties.

I can see now that I probably would have succeeded without business school because drive and ambition have played just as big a role in my success as any academic credential. But I know that I'm far better off—both personally and professionally—with the skills, standards and personal network Tuck provided. (Btw, "personal network" is how MBAs so warmly refer to "their friends.")

I can see now that—at 46—I can't actually see as well as I did when I was 25. But what is very clear is that I was enormously, wildly fortunate to attend Tuck and to have had the great career that followed.

My work mission today is to use humor to help others find success and joy in *their* work lives. I'm beginning this mission where I began my career: with business school. It is my hope that this book provides you, kind reader, with a better framework with which to approach business school, some catalyzed reflection and—most importantly—hearty laughter to help you during the stressful process of considering, applying to and working your way through a top MBA program and your post-graduation career.

A WORD ABOUT COMEDY

N O ONE SPENDS THE MODERN EQUIVALENT OF $150,000 in business school tuition expecting to learn that he wants to be a stand-up comedian, yet that is what happened to me.

During the first semester of my first year at Tuck, I started writing for the student newspaper. My snarky articles in *The Tuck Times* earned me an invitation to co-host the Tuck Talent Show. While I had done some plays in high school and was often cracking jokes in our classes, I had never told jokes in front of an audience before.

I killed.

It was one of the most fun, adrenaline-rich and *natural* experiences of my life. From that point on, I was hooked. I looked for every opportunity to get more of THAT.

I hosted three more talent shows, emceed the Tuck Winter Carnival event, continued writing for the paper and then spoke at our class graduation. All of these were crazy fun.

But what next? I really wanted to get after the comedy thing, but how? I was coming out of business school in 1997 with a staggering amount of student debt. I had landed a gig selling advertising for LAUNCH.com, a music website (that was way before its time), and I decided to throw myself into my job. There was no time to chase the dream. I worked my ass off for four years, as the company rode the roller coaster of the first Dotcom wave, completely unraveling with the rest of the Internet industry in 2001.

After 9/11, a friend said to me, "You know—life is short. If you want do to comedy, you need to go do it." The next day I signed up for comedy lessons at a local theatre in Santa Monica, CA where I was then living.

I started with the lessons, then did open mics and "bringer shows" where a newbie comedian whores out his friends for stage time. God bless my supportive and patient comrades.

Meanwhile, Yahoo! had picked LAUNCH off the scrap heap of the dotcom garbage pile, buying us for change that Jerry Yang found in his couch. And thank God they did because Yahoo! was the best brand on the internet at the time and turned out to be an incredibly fun place to work. I had a blast and learned a ton. Yahoo! yielded positive financial benefits too, as the company's business and stock price rebounded in a huge way under the leadership of our new CEO Terry Semel.

After saving a little money, I finally decided to give that comedy itch a full scratch in 2005. I left Yahoo! and the regular paycheck to work as a comedian full time, hosting several shows almost every weekend at any one of the three Improv comedy clubs in Orange County, CA.

As the emcee for shows headlined by great comics like Bill Burr, Dave Attell, Norm MacDonald, Roseanne Barr and many more, I would do 10 or 15 minutes of material at the top of the show, then bring out the other, much more established (and much funnier) comedians.

Of the many things I learned at the Improv, one was that being good at open mics doesn't mean you were good in the comedy big leagues, which is populated by comics with 5, 10 or 20 years of experience under their belt. One time after I introduced Daniel Tosh, he began his set with "Paul Ollinger—God bless him he's trying." Which was pretty damn funny, and unfortunately true.

But I worked hard, got (a little) better and found my way into some incredibly cool experiences, including performing as the opening act for Jeff Dunham (the ventriloquist who is one of the highest grossing comedians of all-time) when he shot his Comedy Central special, *Spark of Insanity*.

The point here is that I was making progress and having a pretty non-typical post-MBA experience.

I went back to the corporate world in 2007, shortly after I got engaged (to the previously mentioned hot wife), wagering that the little start-up I was going to—Facebook—would have a more positive ROI for my imminent family than working for $20,000/ year and free chicken wings. It did (by a lot).

But I've never been able to shake the comedy bug, and all this time later I'm back doing a few sets per month at the local clubs here in Atlanta. At 46, I'm beginning all over again. And even though I've done over 500 sets of comedy in real clubs in front of real crowds, I'm once again a newcomer who struggles for stage time, a defined point-of-view and a substantive set I'm proud of.

So I'm going to keep pushing forward. Because the only way to get better is to keep doing it, year after year. As Ralphie May said to me once in the Improv green room, "Don't worry, maaaan. You'll start to get the hang of it in about eight years…"

"Eight years?" I thought. "I don't have eight years to get good at this."

Well, that was about eight years ago. So I guess I'm re-starting that clock and making up for lost time in the chicken wing department.

•

CHAPTER 1

YOU SHOULD TOTALLY GET AN MBA

AN MBA IS THE GATEWAY TO AWESOMENESS.

After you obtain this coveted degree, people who would otherwise think less of you will ask, "*You* have an MBA?"

You will reply, "In fact I do."

They will then desire you physically, offer you a job and give you lots of money.

Having—nay, *being*—an MBA will improve your life in ways you have never even considered.

Once you achieve MBA-ness, you will never again experience self-doubt, misunderstanding or halitosis.

Young people will find you captivating. Auto mechanics will take you more seriously. Airline attendants will seat you early and bring you extra peanuts and unlimited Diet Sprites.

Those lacking an MBA will view you as a sorcerer of business… not just as Master of Business Administration but as a Magical Business Animal…a Muscle-Bound Angel…a Much-Beloved Astronaut.

For the MBA is not just a credential. It is a portal to the best version of you, and without it you would be a less-complete human being.

Earning an MBA is like eating every great business book ever written and living them as if they were your own flesh-and-blood.

Once endowed with an MBA, you will awaken the giant within. You will be a great (not good) outlier. You will not sweat the small stuff. You will play liar's poker with the smartest guys in the room and never fear the barbarians at the gate.

And no one—NO ONE—will ever move your fucking cheese.

Okay, I may be exaggerating. Just a tiny, little bit.

Said more accurately, I'm lying. I'm lying through my tea-stained teeth. (I just lied again—they're not stained by tea, they're stained by coffee, cheap merlot and gas station taquitos.)

But I do believe in the MBA degree and experience, which—if done right—will earn you a whole mess o' value. So let's be clear:

- An MBA *will not* give you...
  - Wisdom
  - Ambition
  - Sexual prowess
  - Tact (as I have just proven)

- An MBA *will* give you...
  - Some very solid skills / knowledge
  - A great network/ some open doors
  - A prettier resume

Business school will not only teach you about business, it will teach you how to *think about* business. At top programs, you'll meet great people who will broaden your thinking and raise your standards.

And once finished with your studies, you will have at your disposal super-cool tools like the 2x2 Matrix for strategy, the 4 P's for marketing and that one for finance that I forgot right after I got out of school.

Sure, you've been moderately successful in your career so far, but once you are outfitted with these powerful weapons, you will be an unstoppable business super-hero.

How Did You Get Here?

So it's come to this. You have been out of college for two or three years. Perhaps even two or three times that. Work is going okay... maybe it's even going great. But you want more. You want a change of careers. You want to be on the fast track. Or maybe you just want to learn some cool buzzwords and how to make fancy charts. Understandably, you're thinking that business school might be for you.

Before you rush on off and sign up for the GMAT or the GRE, let's make sure that business school is right for you. Peruse the list of qualifiers below and check all that apply:

❑ My career is stalling.

❑ I want to make more money.

❑ I have exhausted all honest means of making a living.

❑ I want to make more money.

❑ I'm looking for a spouse who knows how to use Excel.[1]

❑ I want to make more money.

❑ I heard MBAs make better lovers.[2]

❑ I want to make more money.

❑ I'm 25, tending bar, blowing beer burps into the face of my future career. My dad recently took me aside for a "come-to-Jesus" discussion. He promised to pay for a GMAT prep course if I could contain the partying just long enough to get through it. He also reminded me that I made decent grades at Ithaca and if he knew I was going to be this kind of a deadbeat, he would have sent me to public school. So the beast within me awoke and declared: "I will make something of my life. I will be someone. I will get—and be—an MBA!"

❑ I want to make more money.

---

1   Not the worst marital criterion I've ever heard.
2   Completely true.

If you answered YES to any (or half) of the questions above, then you should totally go to business school!

On the other hand...

Just as there are very good reasons for going to business school, there are also some pretty bad reasons for going to business school. Given the time and money required to earn an MBA from a top program, anything less than a deep-burning commitment to get an MBA will not suffice.

Here are some common excuses misguided people use to consider pursuing an MBA. You will find many of these on abandoned applications and in the files of mid-year drop-outs.

Please check all that apply:

❑ Just broke up with my boo and am feeling totes sad.

❑ Bored / Nothing better to do.

❑ Will make Mom and/or Dad proud.

❑ I have no idea what to do with my career.

If you checked any of the above, you need to check that gut. Why?

- Feeling sad is best remedied by writing a poem, doing yoga or taking up macramé. Sadness is nowhere near the career motivator that greed is. Come on! (Caveat here is that if being single opens you up to new life experiences and re-establishing yourself as an independent entity, then you're better off without that loser.)

- Bored / Nothing better to do: applying to business school isn't fun—it's a GIGANTIC pain in the ass. If you're not totally fired up about the process, the admissions folks are going to smell stink all over your turd of an application. Do better!

- Similarly, "Need to make Mom/Dad proud" won't get you through…unless they're paying your tuition, in which case, #1—Lucky you (jerk), and #2—Go for it.

- Don't know what to do with my career: we'll discuss this one at length in Chapter 4. For the time being, keep that to yourself.

So, really, who should apply to business school?

There's no one answer. The typical applicant to a top U.S. business school has been out of school a few years, is in her mid-to-late 20's. Her few years since undergrad (where she made good grades and was very involved) have provided "real world" work knowledge and some life lessons, but she's hungry to accelerate her career and/or build her skillset so she can set out on her own.

Another applicant might have been in the Peace Corps or the Army, and is now looking to optimize his entry into the corporate world with the MBA credential, knowledge and network. Others are those with undergrad majors in Chemistry, English or Sociology who want to gain a mastery of business skills so that they can climb the management ladder.

Should you decide to go to business school, your classmates will come from a multitude of professions and countries all around the world. They will include not just bankers and consultants, but PhD's, chefs, entrepreneurs, engineers, salespeople, sky-divers, jugglers, singers and—yes—even lawyers. You might go to school with an Olympic skier from Lake Tahoe, the son of a Korean billionaire or a woman who grew up in poverty in one of the poorest areas of Mexico City.

Whatever the resume, these applicants are looking for a way to take their careers to the next level. And they know that business school can be an amazing springboard to help them get there.

FAMOUS BUSINESS PEOPLE WHO DO NOT HAVE AN MBA

Bill Gates, Founder of Microsoft

Oprah Winfrey, Media Magnate

Mark Zuckerberg, CEO/Co-founder, Facebook

Larry Ellison, Founder/CEO, Oracle

Marc Benioff, Founder/CEO, Salesforce.com

Each of these people is a corporate behemoth who created an empire, employs thousands of people and donates many millions to charitable causes.

Can you *imagine* what they could have accomplished if they had gone to business school?

(I almost feel sorry for them.)

Business School v. Law School

If you are considering business school, there is a reasonable chance that you are also considering other graduate programs to enhance your career. You may even be considering going to law school (you poor thing). Here are several reasons why business school is better than law school:

- Business school is 33% shorter than law school, which means 33% fewer classes, 33% less tuition, 33% fewer years of foregone income.

- No Bar Exam or Continuing Legal Education (CLE). When you graduate from business school, you *are* an MBA and you are free to "practice business." Chump law school grads still have to pass the Bar Exam to practice law. Suckas.

- B-school guys are less douchy than law school guys.[3] If you are in the market for a fella, then you'll do great at b-school, which is a hot dog fest for smart, motivated dudes. It's not as male-heavy as it used to be, but it's still like shooting sausage in a barrel.

- B-school women are cooler and better looking than law school women. (I have no data to support this, but I feel pretty good about it as unsubstantiated conjecture.)

- Most importantly: when it's all over, you won't have to be a lawyer.

Here's where I confess that, before I applied to business school, I was considering doing a joint JD-MBA program. I took the LSAT, but bombed it. I thereby decided I would go to a great business school instead of a crappy joint degree program. Net: the LSAT saved me an additional two years of school and a lifetime of being a lawyer.

---

3   Your results may differ...especially if you go to Wharton.

CHAPTER 2

MBA CAREERS

WHEN YOUR BUSINESS SCHOOL DEAN TOUCHES YOU UPON the shoulders with your diploma, he confers upon you both the MBA and access to career opportunities that you will hardly believe.

Investment banking. Brand management. Strategy consulting. These are super-fancy and lucrative jobs for which you are eligible only after learning the secret MBA handshake.

As your graduation date looms closer, legions of senior recruiters from top companies in these industries will flock to your campus to try to persuade you to come work for them.

Why?

Because you are a budding MBA and that makes you *almost* awesome! (I told you it was great to be an MBA…I was only lying a little.)

But if you were like me when I was considering business school (earnest yet naïve, and clad in ill-fitting, triple-pleated khakis), you probably don't know about all the great opportunities awaiting you post-MBA.

I remained clueless long after getting into Tuck (some would say long after graduation). In fact, a few weeks after matriculating (which is a fancy way of saying I showed up to school for first year), I went to the career services office and threw myself at the feet of my job search jungle guides, one of the great services provided by the top schools.

"Guys, school has barely started but all my classmates seem to already know what they're going to do with their careers. I don't even know what a consultant does!"

"Relax," they assured me. "No one knows what consultants do" (at the very least, they were pretty damn funny).

To help you get a couple of steps ahead of where I was in the career enlightenment process, please enjoy the following in-depth explanation of the glamorous jobs that await you on the other side of that MBA graduation. The above-averageness of these jobs will blow your mind!

MBA JOBS EXPLAINED

- **Brand Management:** This is another name for marketing, i.e. the science of tricking people into buying products. It's a rewarding, relatively cozy career track if you can land yourself at a P&G, Pepsico, General Mills or a few other blue chip companies. Of course you may end up in the marketing training program for a pesticide manufacturer or some shitty mattress retailer. They'll pay you okay, but it's not going to get you laid.

- **Consulting:** Career in which you leave your house on Sunday night, fly to Iowa to count bovine carcasses hanging in a meat locker. You analyze the meat-killing process that got said dead cows hanging there in the first place, write a report that supports the meat-killing/ hanging strategy that the meat-killing client already had. Client then uses your report to lay off a bunch of meat-killing employees while paying your firm a bunch of dough. Then you wake up one morning and realize you have burned 2/80ths of your expected lifespan on a project that essentially encourages humans to consume more red meat. The downside of consulting is that your life is a grind and you never see your friends or family. The upside is that you make awesome money to pay off your school loans and get one more "Smarty Pants" badge on your résumé.

- **Digital Juggernauts:** Google, Facebook, Amazon, Apple. These are the equivalent of going to work at IBM or

Coke in the '80s, but with free lunch, foosball tables and entitled Millennials (sorry—that phrase is redundant). These are the leading corporations of our day. They are awesome for your résumé and you will earn a handsome salary with wonderful benefits. The funny equity money has been off the table for a while at these places, so the opportunity is about skills, market knowledge and networking. It can be pretty cool to work at a place where you might sit next to a billionaire in the cafeteria…for a little while. Enjoy your time on this assignment until you muster the stomach to start your own thing.

- **Investment Banking:** A lucrative career for those with a knack for finance, a drive to be the best and a gigantic ego. The early years in investment banking are exhilarating and exhausting. You work around the clock to produce long, detailed proposals (pitch decks) for some client to buy some other company for an exorbitant sum. The technical term for this entry role is "Deck Bitch" (hey, don't blame *me* for this sexism on Wall Street). Does the acquisition make sense? Doesn't matter! Any transaction generates massive fees for your employer and a big, fat year-end bonus for you. (Capitalism is so awesome.) At some point after five years or so you will realize that you are on a treadmill on which you will be stuck until you retire or die from a heart attack. But you'll die rich.

- **Hedge Fund Management:** The richest dudes and dudettes (but mostly dudes) in finance. Their 2/20 rule means they get paid a 2% management fee plus 20% of the profits that their funds generate. Technically known as having their cake and eating it too, this is very good for the partners at the hedge fund (assuming there are any profits) and assuming they don't end up in jail for insider trading.

- **Private Equity (PE):** *Most* PE folks are lovely people, but *some* are ravenous sharks who buy businesses, fire half the employees, then sell them (the company, not the employees…well, okay, they do sell a third of the employees) to some other party for a lot more money. This is what Mitt Romney did at Bain and it's where the work of Adam Smith and Charles Darwin intersect.

FAMOUS MBA CRIMINALS

Jeffrey Skilling (HBS), former CEO of Enron, found guilty of conspiracy, insider trading, securities fraud and more! The smartest guy in the room. Er, cell.

Michael Milken (Wharton), Junk Bond King, pled guilty to securities fraud, fined $600 million. But his biggest crime was the toupee he wore doing all that insider trading stuff.

Anil Kumar (Wharton), **Raj Rajaratnam** (Wharton), **Rajat Gupta** (HBS) amazingly brilliant and accomplished businessmen who were all found guilty for insider trading. Because being merely filthy rich wasn't enough.

- **Start-ups:** The professional equivalent of buying a lottery ticket. Going to work at a small tech company, most likely in San Francisco, New York, Austin, Silicon Valley, Los Angeles or Atlanta (if you screwed up). The free lunches, unlimited t-shirts and frequent happy hours are great, and it's pretty darn cool to be on a mission with friends to disrupt [*insert name of industry that doesn't need to be disrupted*]. That is, until the whole thing comes crashing down around you, driving you to doubt yourself, resent your colleagues and make bad short-term decisions regarding personal relationships. So just know that while you may win the lottery, it's more likely that you'll end up with a big goose egg at the end of it. Good luck using those free lunches to pay your school loans.

- **Management Analyst:** *US News* describes this career thusly: "In this field, you'll leverage data and provide feedback on improving an organization's efficiency and profitability." *Zzzzzzzzzz.* Is one of the job requirements "praying for your own death"?

- **Petroleum Engineer** or **Software Developer (insert name of "your old job"):** You're not going to learn how to do be either of these at b-school, which means you must have brought some of this knowledge to school with you. So if you already had employable skills, why did you bother going to business school in the first place? It was very selfish of you to take the spot of some other student who had nothing to offer before her MBA.

- **The Entertainment Industry:** By this, I mean television or film, not prostitution (though the similarities are undeniable and not coincidental). Lots of USC, UCLA, HBS and NYU folks will end up in marketing, strategic planning or corporate finance in the entertainment biz (btw, if you say "biz," there's a high likelihood that you are a giant d-bag). These jobs pay okay, but not Wall Street or consulting money. Basically, you'll be paid like an entry level brand manager, but be expected to dress like George Clooney. Very few of these companies recruit on-campus, so you're going to have to sell yourself to them (see comment above about prostitution).

- **Pharmaceutical / Medical Device Industry:** You're going to tell a doctor how to treat her patients? You—the person who gave up on a career in science in 10th grade

Biology when you couldn't keep all that mitosis/meiosis stuff straight? You—the person whose greatest scientific accomplishment in college was making a bong out of an apple? You—the person who still treats his own body like a fraternity garbage can? But now, because there is a pile of dough in it, you're going to hang out in doctors' offices, give the staff pens, Frisbees and Post-Its emblazoned with the name of your company's artificial hip and then *actually participate* in the surgery of unsuspecting baby boomers as your widget becomes part of their body? Wow. While this is obviously scary on many levels, just think: business school made all this possible without you wasting eight long years learning how to be a doctor. MBA! MBA!!!

- **Venture Capital:** Basically the same as the music business in that some folks have or raise a pot of money. They then take that money and invest it in, say, 10 companies. Of those companies (the theory goes) one will be a big hit, two will break even, and the other seven will all be a massive waste of time. The big hit pays for the losers, who are treated as such. VCs have the ~~balls~~ gumption to tell businesspeople with decades of experience in an industry VCs know nothing about how to do their jobs. Nothing wins respect and friendship like being a know-it-all who has never had a real job in his life. Remember the golden rule: she with the gold makes the rules. Remember also: there's more than one person out there with gold.

- **Bond Trader:** For those who want to make a bunch o' dough but don't have the brains to get into investment banking, hedge funds or venture capital, trading is a great alternative. Traders can still say that they work at Goldman-Sachs or JP Morgan to impress their dates, and while their banking friends are doing actual work late into the night, traders are at a bar in Tribeca doing lines and shots with buy-side guys (their customers). Before you agree to pursue trading, read *Ghosts of Manhattan* by Douglas Brunt to understand what it feels like to be 35 years old and have your human value conflated with both macroeconomic conditions outside of your control and the amount of cocaine you can shove up your nose.

- **Non-Profit:** A career that truly lives up to its name. As in other industries, the quality of the people and organizations in non-profit vary greatly. Many do amazing work that truly improves the world. Others are every bit as political as the thorniest corporate entities. While you can actually make a very good living in non-profit, you're never going to get rich from your salary alone. If you like to do good but also like expensive wine and Italian designer shoes, consider augmenting your charity-based salary with that of a spouse who is on Wall Street.

- **Wealth Management / Private Client Services:** This is where rich people entrust you with their money to invest, and your company takes a big chunk as a management fee. What if you lose a ton of their money? Doesn't matter—they still owe you the fee (crazy, but so true!). If you can spout portfolio theory with a straight face and deal with the bratty, entitled heirs to someone else's fortune, this is a great job for you.

- **Sales (any kind):** Are you kidding me? You don't need an MBA to do that. Have some self-respect already! If you can't find any other work, do what you have to do, I guess. But you're going to have to lie to your parents and tell them that you're "in Business Development" so they can salvage some dignity at the country club.

- **Business Development:** BD guys/women are just bad sales people who take good notes. They think they've closed a deal when they get an NDA signed. They wear

31

pleated khakis with blue oxford button downs or maybe a striped oxford button down if they're feeling extra wacky that day. They talk about frameworks a lot.

- **Stand-up Comedian:** Tell jokes that killed in business school to crowds of the general public who sit there, stare at you and say audibly, "this guy sucks ass." Get paid in chicken wings for 10 years before anyone recognizes your genius. Live in constant doubt as to whether you'll ever earn enough to survive. As you cry yourself to sleep, keep repeating to yourself, "But I have an Ivy League MBA…"

| WHAT YOUR CLASSMATES WILL BE DOING IN 10 YEARS ||
FIRST JOB OUT OF SCHOOL	WHAT THEY'LL BE DOING IN 10 YEARS
Investment Banking Analyst	CFO of mid-sized company
Brand Management	Consulting
Consulting	Brand Management
Hedge Fund Analyst	Hard Time
Venture Capital	Waiting for the first fund to pay out, counting chickens on the second fund that won't pay out for another eight years
Sales	Anything he has to do to hit his number
Real Estate	Calling you out of the blue to talk about a deal he's putting together (ie. looking to borrow your money to buy some dirt)
Social Enterprise Manager	Making lattes at the YMCA
Hot Shit Start-up	Sitting in an expensive house on an expensive couch, wondering what the hell to do with their life now that they don't have to pay the mortgage

CHAPTER 3

SO, LIKE,
WHERE DO I
START?

OKAY, PAUL—YOU'VE CONVINCED ME, YOU SAY TO yourself. I really want one of those great jobs and I know I have to go to business school to get one. So, like, where do I start?

You *have* started—you're reading my book after all! That puts you way further along than the dirty cretins you're competing against.

But now it's really important to make sure your first moves count. Don't just dial up the HBS admissions office and say, "Hey, I've decided I'll come to Harvard. When does school start?"

That's not how it works, Bud Fox. You are now at the beginning of a long journey, and you have to prepare yourself before you set off.

Here's what you've got to do:

1. Wade in coolly
2. Learn the admissions game language
3. Get your story straight
   a. Take stock
   b. Know what you bring to the party
   c. Do the research
4. Get GMAT-ready

1. Wade in Coolly

Have you ever seen that movie where two love-struck teenagers announce gleefully to all who will listen that they are in love and are getting married? Meanwhile the grown-ups are all like, "…and when did you decide this?"

You saw that movie, right?

The issue is not that these grown-ups are dead inside and haven't had great sex in years (though that is a distinct possibility).

No, it's that these grown-ups understand the kids' decision comes from their impulsive hearts and impetuous genitals, instead of from the methodical thinking and reasoning of a mature, joyless brain.

My point is this: just because you've decided you want to go to business school, don't just start blabbing about it to everyone before you do some prep work. You've got to get your feet wet with self-reflection, research and inquiry about the right program for you, how you get in and what it takes to actually graduate.

So *do* wade in coolly and let your body and brain acclimate to the water of this new journey. Start by understanding your own motivation and goals.

Remember that time in high school before you had your driver's license when you and your buddy took your parents' car out for a cruise? And then when you got home with a trunk full of illegal fireworks, your neighbor's mailbox and 24 empty Rolling Rocks, your dad was standing there in the driveway waiting for you?[4]

That happened to you too, right? Either way, remember (or try to imagine) the lesson here—before you start talking, GET YOUR STORY STRAIGHT.

Start getting your story together by learning what business school is all about. Research what business school can do for your career. Understand the business school environment. Get clear on the logistics of applying, and learn about the schools themselves.

Pay attention to what makes each school special, different, unique (if only in their own minds). Think through the location and environment where you'd like to study. And figure out—realistically—what you have to offer in return.

If you do this, you will come across as informed, thoughtful and purposeful. If you do not do this, you will come across like a foolhardy moron.

---

4   You probably don't want to mention this in your essays or interviews.

2. Learn the Admissions Game Language
(utter not "MBA School")

Like the mob, business schools have developed their own proprietary terminology so that they can identify those who are "friends of theirs." If you want to be taken seriously by business school admissions teams—or not end up locked in a mobster's trunk—you have to speak the language.

Just as a child's vocabulary expands with exposure to his environment, so will your fluency grow as you expose yourself to the world of post-graduate business education (please do not take "expose yourself" literally here).

The very first linguistic nuance to adopt is this: you are seeking admission to "business school," not to "MBA school."

Just typing those words here is painful.

Saying "MBA school" is like saying "diploma school." Doctors don't go to "MD school." Lawyers don't go to "JD school." So bad-ass future holders of the MBA don't go to "MBA school." They go to business school.

Even the quite popular truncation "b-school" should be used in moderation. Over-usage of "b-school" makes you sound like one of those people who call The Bay Area "'Frisco" or "SF." God, just shut up. You're not even talking but you're already annoying me.

Net: using the phrase "MBA school" is the verbal equivalent of picking your nose in your admissions interview, eating that juicy booger then exclaiming "Deelish!" to the horrified university employee who just witnessed the cataclysm of your ignorance.

Take your shoddy overalls and bare feet back to the fields, Jethro. There is no room for you here in our hallowed halls.

The "MBA school" mistake is just one example of myriad potential pitfalls that await the uninformed. To help you get up to speed on all the critical terms, I have prepared the following non-exhaustive glossary of Business School Admissions Terms.

"*In six more weeks, these M.B.A.s will be ready for market.*"

BUSINESS SCHOOL ADMISSION TERMS

Acceptance Rate: The % of applicants that a school admits for a given year's class. *Acceptance Rate = Total # Accepted / Total Applicants* (if you can't follow this math, don't apply to business school).

AdCom: The Admissions Committee, i.e. the group of people who pick the members of the incoming class for the top schools, and the answer to the (hopefully) rhetorical question, "Who do I have to blow to get into HBS?"

Cohort: The portion of your class (generally 50-90 students) with whom you take your core classes. They will witness your first cold-call and inevitable pants-crapping. And you shall witness theirs.

Cold Call: When a professor calls on you in class to answer a question. See also "crap your pants."

The Consortium: A group of schools banded together to enhance diversity in business education. Members include

Tuck, Berkeley, UCLA, Carnegie-Mellon, Cornell, Emory, Georgetown, Indiana, Michigan, NYU, UNC, USC, Texas, Darden, Wash U, Wisconsin and Yale. If you are a white or Asian dude, this probably isn't going to help you.

EA / Early Admission: If you are not a slam-dunk at your top school, you need to do the early admissions thing. You committing to attend early means they can maintain a low acceptance rate, which is a metric of exclusivity.

Essays: The exhibition of your soul for the sadistic entertainment of the admissions committee. Make 'em interesting and personal or you're not getting in. Limit profanity where possible.

Financial Aid: The grants, loans and scholarships that help make your MBA possible. See also "years of Ramen noodles" and "Indentured Servitude."

GMAT: Mind-bender of a skills assessment test on which your future as an MBA depends highly. Not as hard as some of the other graduate school admissions tests, but you'll need to prepare for it (see Chapter 10).

Ivy League: A collection of eight prestigious universities in the Northeastern United States (Harvard, Yale, Dartmouth, Columbia, Cornell, Univeristy of Pennsylvania, Princeton and Brown). The last two don't have proper business schools, which means you shouldn't trust them.

Lecture v. Case Method: Either a professor drones on endlessly about how smart she is about a given topic (lecture) or she makes you prove you actually read the assigned stories about business people dealing with any variety of issues at their businesses (case method). Some cases are really interesting and informative. Others are just boring as all hell.

Legacy: Child or nephew or niece of some rich alumnus/-a. A legacy's GMAT might have been 550, but his credit score is

CHAPTER 3

850, so he's getting in. Reminder: life isn't fair. The sooner you embrace this concept, the happier you will be in the long run (and by "happier," I mean "less disappointed").

M7 (Magnificent 7): Clique-y alliance of top schools, including HBS, Stanford, Wharton, MIT, Columbia, Kellogg and Chicago. The pajama-clad leadership of these schools have sleepovers at each others' campuses, brush each other's hair, throw pillow fights and write in a slam book about the schools that aren't in the M7. It's super cute.

Math Camp: A pre-enrollment class / review of calculus and accounting for those lacking in deep quantitative skills and experience. Don't set your academic expectations from this experience, as the heavy-hitters will not be in attendance (see "Poet"). By the way, the vast majority of your classmates at top programs will be brilliant, poised and diligent. But don't be surprised when you meet a dipshit or two. A few get by the AdComs at even the top schools every year.

Opportunity Cost: In this case, how much money you would have made / the fun you would have had / what you could have done with that tuition $ if you didn't go to business school. It's the concept you're addressing when you repeatedly bang your head against the wall and moan, "What the hell am I doing with my life?"

Pass / Fail: A class where grading is all or nothing. If you can't muster the effort to actually pass one of these classes, you really deserve that F.

Pit-Divers: Ass-kissing class members who clamor up to the professor after class, feigning interest in her wisdom or tie. All they're really interested in is better grades. These are the future consultants.

Poet: A cute nickname for a student who is bad at math. It sounds nice and romantic, but when someone calls you a poet, they are insulting you.

40

Quant / Quant Jock: A student who is really good at math (and sometimes bad at showering). Be friends with her because you're going to need her help with your homework.

Section: see "Cohort."

Study Groups: The small team of people with whom you will complete most of your out-of-class assignments, and something for which you must profess sincere excitement in your essays and interviews, even if you hate other people. These classmates will know in short-order whether or not you are smart.

Tuition: Mindboggling sum that is table stakes for the right to work your fingers to the bone to earn the MBA. Money well spent!

ADMISSIONS GLOSSARY 2— SCHOOL NICKNAMES

Most top business schools are named for a kindly rich person who gave the school a bunch of moolah. Some of these benefactors' names have become the school's de facto identity (e.g. saying "Wharton" is at least as common as saying "Penn") while others are less familiar…perhaps because they hardly roll off the tongue (e.g. The University of Texas at Austin McCombs School of Business).

Knowing and using these nicknames will make you more fluent in the language *du* business school.

Anderson: Anderson is the very good b-school at UCLA. It's in LA, baby! So if you love sunshine, have your people call their people and put this highly selective program on your list.

Booth: University of Chicago's brand name. Not named for John Wilkes Booth (because that would be very weird...and because JWB didn't have the $300 million to spare that Chicago alum David Booth had).

CBS: Columbia Business School or America's most-watched television network, the home of the "#1 drama/scripted program (*NCIS*); #1 sitcom (*THE BIG BANG THEORY*); #1 newsmagazine (*60 MINUTES*)."

Darden: Name of University of Virginia's prestigious school, and also the name of the company that owns the prestigious Olive Garden restaurant. However, there is no affiliation between the two. Darden was named for Colgate Whitehead Darden Jr., a former congressman and president of UVA. Just think—Darden could have been named "Whitehead."

Fuqua: Duke University's business school. Be sure you pronounce that first syllable with a hard "U" (FYOO-kwaa). Get it wrong, and you will fuq yourself right out of a chance to join this prestigious institution.

GSB: Short-hand for Stanford's Graduate School of Business. It's one of many annoyingly-redundant acronyms you're going to have to learn to appear informed. Chicago also uses "GSB," but more commonly goes by "Booth."

Goizueta: The hard to pronounce business school at Emory University in Atlanta, named for former Coca-Cola CEO, Roberto Goizueta.

Haas: UC Berkeley's fine business school, named for Walter Haas, a former head honcho at Levi Strauss & Co. Levi Strauss himself endowed 28 Berkeley scholarships in 1897. Wear jeans to your interview.

HBS: Acronym for Harvard Business School. They call it HBS because it's easier to spell.

Johnson: This Johnson would be Cornell's business school.

Kellogg: Northwestern's highly-esteemed school o' business. A cereal joke here would be trite and hackneyed. It would not be Grrreat!!!! (I'm sorry.)

Kelley: Indiana University's fine business school, located in Bloomington, IN. Not to be confused with Keller School of Management at DeVry University, located online or at a highway exit near you.

Kenan-Flagler: UNC's hyphenated b-school, named for the families who brought us both Union-Carbide and Standard Oil. Go Heels!

Marshall: Business school at University of Southern California. To gain admission, one must know all the words to Fleetwood Mac's "Tusk."

McCombs: University of Texas at Austin's business school nickname, in honor of Red McCombs. "Oh that is so cute—a feller named 'Red' from Texas got himself a business school!" you think in your haughty New England sweater until you learn that Red McCombs is a business titan of monumental proportions and you would be lucky to be his assistant's assistant, you prep school prick!

McDonough: Georgetown's business school, perched high on the banks of the Thames. Sorry, I mean the Potomac. The Thames is someplace else. London, maybe. Yeah, it's in London (according to Wikipedia).

Olin: The school of business at Washington University, which makes its home in St. Louis. The 'Lou is also home to many national hip hop acts, including Nelly, Chingy, J-Kwon and Murphy Lee.

Owen: Vanderbilt's School of Business. Even with Nashville's low cost of living, tuition is high so that when it's all over you'll be Owen' sum money (I'm sorry 2.0).

Ross: Michigan's business school's name, in honor of Stephen Ross, a real estate magnate who has given U of M over $300 million (and counting). Mr. Ross is chairman of The Related Companies, and if you're related to him, you are either very rich or very jealous (or both).

Sloan: It sounds like the name of a sultry, slightly-drugged-out heiress socialite, but it is actually the name of the business school at MIT.

Stern: NYU's b-school. It's in the middle of Greenwich Village. Most students wear berets and smoke clove cigarettes during class.

Tepper: B-school at Carnegie Mellon University in Pittsburgh. It is far-and-away the best business school in all of western Pennsylvania, eastern Ohio and northern West Virginia.

Tuck: Dartmouth's prestigious business school, which is only open to the smartest and best-looking applicants. This is where the MBA was invented and perfected. You would be damn lucky to get in here. N.B.: Tuck has no affiliation with Tuck's Medicated Cooling Pads for hemorrhoids (you'll learn more about these as you get older).

Wharton: University of Pennsylvania's much-acclaimed business school. Wharton undergrads (who also go to Wharton) use the name to trick people who don't know the difference between a BA and an MBA.

3. Do Your Research

Now that you have a firm grasp on the basic language of MBA admissions, it's time to dive deeper on the specifics of the top MBA programs themselves.

Here's how you get started:

1. **Buy some business school guidebooks.** The best one to recommend to your friends: *You Should Totally Get an MBA* by Paul Ollinger (oh wait, you're reading it now, so you know how good it is). Be sure to tweet and share the highly entertaining and substantive content to your millions of social media followers. For a very readable narrative description of the business school experience, check out Philip Delves Broughton's *Ahead of the Curve: Two Years at Harvard Business School*. Broughton recounts how he, a journalist, fought his way into and through HBS, despite lacking quantitative skills and the presumption that income maximization is the secret to happiness. Though he considers himself grateful for the HBS experience and degree, his observations of life at one of the very best MBA programs in the world raise questions about business school culture and priorities that are worth your full consideration.

2. **Get online.** In truth, there really aren't that many MBA program guidebooks any more. The data you want are online. Check out these information-rich destinations:

    a. **Poets&Quants.com** is a great source (kind of *the* source) for in-depth research into and current news about business schools and the admissions process. Lots of testimonials from current and former applicants. Lots of advice from admissions committee folks and industry experts.

    b. **GMATclub.com** is a very useful tool that includes user-generated discussions and sub-threads that allow you to tap the collective intelligence of applicants,

45

current students and alumni. It's pretty fascinating to read other applicants' stories, especially those with high GMAT scores / high GPAs who didn't get into their first choice school(s).

c. **Major Rankings**—each with a different slant or methodology are available from *The Economist, US News, Financial Times, BusinessWeek* and *Forbes*. Rankings are useful directional data, but take them with a grain of salt. Some of the funniest and most useful information herein includes the user comments below the articles. Alumni tend to get super-offended when their programs slip in the rankings. And there are few things funnier than a pissed-off MBA.

3. **School Websites.** Visit the websites of the top schools or the schools you think you might want to apply to. There's all kinds of info and webinars and stuff on their sites. All of them are going to tell you that they're global, diverse, green, ethical and collaborative (whatever). Beyond that, they'll share their unique strengths, values and admission criteria. These are how they position themselves in the market so you will eventually have to sell your yourself vis-à-vis their positioning (regardless of how delusional either party may be).

4. **Talk to friends.** Hey, it's a social world. Sure, you could crowd-source this information-gathering by Facebook posting, "I'm going to business school! Where should I go y'all?" But that's not super smart or thoughtful. So arrange to have coffee or grab a beer with a friend who has been to business school and pick her brain.

5. **Talk to friends of friends.** There is so much networking in the business world that you might as well start practicing the art now. Didn't your friend's brother go to Wharton? By all means, reach out to him (unless you hooked up with him and barfed on his shoes once).

6. **Get Linky With It:** LinkedIn is your new best friend. Dig around to see which of your connections went to what schools. You might run across a profile or two and think, "That knucklehead has an MBA?" Don't worry—he was probably a legacy.

Early Networking: Ask Good Questions

At this early stage, the people you talk to about going to school will not expect you to be an expert on their alma mater or business school in general, but they are still potentially influential to your admission.

Embrace the opportunity to demonstrate your sincere, semi-informed curiosity with some insightful questions.

Note that many people whom you talk to at this stage will ask you why you want to go to school. You aren't yet at the point to where you need to give an essay-ready answer, but sharing even a germ of an idea is better than having none or saying "I want to make more money," even if that *is* one of the key motivating factors (see Chapter 11: *It's Not About the Money (Yes it is)*).

Here are some questions you can ask:

- Why did you go to business school?
- Would you go again?
- What were your classmates like?
- What kind of work are your classmates doing?
- What was the dating / family scene like at your school?[5]
- You make boatloads of cash, right?[6]

---

5   The business school experience is way different for those who have kids v. those who are still swinging singles.
6   Don't ask this. But you can ask, "Did your MBA pay off financially?"

The answers to some of the questions above might actually help you formulate your own answers. Note: I did not say to *steal* their answers…just, you know, *borrow* the ones you really like.

ALUMNI v. ALUMNUS v. ALUMNA v. ALUMNAE

Indulge a quick Latin lesson to help you avoid looking like a doofus.

Alumnus and *Alumna* are Latin words meaning "former student," respectively male and female.

Alumnae is a plural form of the feminine.

Alumni is a plural form of the masculine. It can also mean more than one male and female former students.

This lesson in a dead language serves to help you avoid a very common error among the unwashed, i.e. referring to individual people as "alumni."

Just like the "MBA School" gaffe, it seems innocuous enough, but it isn't. It is the kind of error that makes potential advocates and admissions officers roll their eyes and think, "oh Lord, another one of these…"

Don't be that guy/gal. Be the guy/gal who knows the difference.

Not that you have to be a dick about it…

Get Your Story Straight: Take Stock 1
WHY are you doing this (like, for real)?

Before you are admitted to a top business school program, you will be asked a thousand times—in a thousand different ways—why you want to get your MBA. Your story has to add up. This is where those informational coffee sessions with friends of friends come in handy—because they help you synthesize your story.

More importantly, your reasoning should mean something to you. Like, something real.

Greed and dumb jokes aside, there are plenty of other ways to blow 2 years of your life and $150,000. Sure, business school can be fun, but with that kind of time and dough, why not go on a mission in Africa? Or, better yet, why not launch a 21-month bender in Thailand?

So seriously, *why are you doing this?*

You might as well figure out what's really motivating you here. Because it's not just a question on an application, it's a question of how you want to spend the rarest of commodities—your time on this planet.

Remember that this is a journey, and the first step is deciding what you want out of the journey. So you've gotta get clear on the following:

- What do you want to do with you life? Really, like, what's your dream? If you could do anything, what would it be?

- How does getting an MBA help you achieve that goal?

- Why do you want to go to the individual school you're talking about or applying to? Like, what things about that program make it a better fit for you and your dreams?

Be honest with yourself. Start writing this stuff down. You don't have to know all the answers yet, but having sincere, well-reasoned goals will not only impress interviewers and essay readers, it will help crystallize a vision for the kind of life you want to live. No joke!

Don't worry if your reasons aren't super lofty, of the "I want to work for the Gates Foundation to help cure malaria" type (though that is certainly a worthwhile goal). But they do need to be interesting and personal. They do need to demonstrate that you are a thinking, self-motivated person who has ideas and a vision for what you want from the world and what you want to contribute in return.

If they are thoughtful and personal, your answers will not be boring. And that's good because on a business school application, boring equals death.

Well, maybe not death, but you won't get in.

WHO CAN I TELL THAT I'M APPLYING TO BUSINESS SCHOOL?

Should I tell my boss / colleague? It depends. Do you trust them? You may need their help with letters of recommendation, but you have to be certain that your colleagues won't use this information against you ("You should promote me over Susan because she's applying to business school right now and will be gone in nine months.") This really isn't a joke. There are some manipulative assholes out there.

Should I tell my friends? As long as they're not colleagues, sure. They'll figure it out soon enough because once you get into the process you are going to be either so motivated or depressed they're going to want to know what the hell has gotten into you.

Should I tell an attractive person I'm trying to sleep with? Absolutely! (That is, if this person seems likely to be impressed by it.) Who am I to tell you to leave your best game at home? Hell, while you're at it, tell them you're curing cancer and producing a movie with that short guy from *The Hunger Games* with the killer abs. Whatever it takes, my friend!

Get your story straight: Take Stock 2
What do you bring to the party (like, for real)?

When it comes to business school applications, remember that you are a product. A unique, brilliant, sexy, motivated product. But still, a product. (If you market yourself well, someday you might even become a brand!)

As in all commerce, the customer (in this case, the b-school AdCom) is looking for products that suit their needs. And there is much competition for their business.

Part of honing your application process is to understand who you need to be in the eyes of these customers. Learn the attributes that schools look for in general, and where you will fall on the spectrum of available products (other human beings who are applying for the same seat you are...):

- **College GPA**

- **GMAT score**

- **College Extracurriculars**: Meaning "involvement/ leadership," not keg stands.

- **Community involvement since college**: E.g. volunteerism, belonging to boards, catalyzing positive social change, etc.

- **Language proficiency**: Note—"American" is not a language.

- **Management experience**: Note—having an assistant is not management.

- **Career progress:** This means things like being promoted, being given more responsibility/budget, taking on new challenges, etc. Note that "not being fired for almost two years" is not the kind of progress AdComs have in mind.

- **Interesting, unique talents / experiences:**
  - o Did you spend a year in India working on a municipal water project? See, that's interesting (if only for the tales of dysentery).
  - o Are you an heir to a massive fortune? You should mention this...subtly, of course, but in a way that can't be missed. It's almost as interesting as the India water project, but with far less intestinal discomfort, and admissions teams love really rich applicants.

So seriously—do you juggle? Do you do magic? Even though this means that you could be a gigantic dork, it makes you different. It helps your application stand out among the other highly-accomplished, highly-motivated people who are competing with you for a seat in that b-school class. Make no mistake—these people are either doing everything they can to make themselves appear more interesting than they actually are, or are actually very interesting. This latter group are the bastards you have to look out for. These applicants speak six languages, have Olympic medals and have seen combat (I don't mean *Mortal Kombat*). Bring your best game.

4. Get GMAT Ready

Take a GMAT practice test: While it may be harder or easier than entrance exams for other graduate programs, the GMAT is a proctology exam of an assessment test. So bend over, relax and understand:

- To get into a top program, you're going to have to score high on the GMAT (or the GRE...but this will be discussed in Chapter 9).

- Since it's very difficult to cheat on the GMAT, you're actually going to have to either: 1) be a genius or 2) study like crazy. If you've read this far in this book, it's pretty clear that #1 does not apply. So, you'd better start studying.

- Your competition is smart and out there studying (those industrious wankers). You should be too.

- At this early stage, take a practice test and assess where you might kinda probably score if you took the test today. Doing so early gives you the chance to spend several months attending GMAT classes and taking additional practice tests. It will inform you on how you should prioritize your study time.

So now you're asking yourself: are GMAT classes fun?

YOU BETCHA! In the same way that a root canal or IRS audit is fun.

In reality, studying for the GMAT is a tedious, soul-killing drag. But it is only one of dozens of drags necessary to get into a top program. If you can't hack the GMAT class, now's a good time to decide you don't want to go to business school.

NOTE: when I was studying for the GMAT, I had more time than money, so I decided to forego the class and bought a few of the much more affordable test guide/practice test books, and just worked those books for dozens of hours at my kitchen table. It worked out fine. Whether you take a class or do the guidebooks thing, the key to success is putting in the time and doing the work. There are some great, free resources online at Khan Academy to get you started. If you can afford it, take the class. Like having a personal trainer or a therapist, it's going to help force you to do the work.

We will discuss the GMAT at length in a subsequent chapter. For now, please accept the paraphrased advice of Harold Geneen, the late CEO of the late conglomerate ITT[7]: "The drudgery of the [studying] will set you free."[8]

---

7   It still exists as a smaller entity today, but it was gigantic back in the day.
8   He actually said "numbers" in reference to how important it is to understand your organization's finances.

CHAPTER 4

FINDING THE RIGHT CAREER FOR YOU

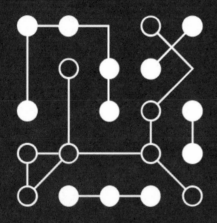

I F YOU DON'T KNOW EXACTLY WHAT JOB YOU WANT AFTER business school, you're not alone. A whopping 64% of the class of 2012 changed careers (according to *BloombergBusiness*[9]). So know that many of your fellow applicants are looking to change careers, even if they won't admit it. This is all perfectly natural—business school provides a great opportunity to learn about lots of different industries and job functions. It's also a great time to develop and reflect upon how your personal skillset and passions would fit there.

Deciding which post-MBA career to pursue can be intimidating. If you're doing it right, the process brings you face-to-face with your strengths, weaknesses and—scariest of all—your dreams.

You can spend thousands of dollars and hundreds of hours pondering the color of your parachute, whining about your "true calling"[10] and taking skills assessments tests like Myers-Briggs and StrengthsFinders.

But you don't need any of that crap because:

1. The answer is already within you, and

2. Your Uncle Paul has the perfect (FREE) tool for you to uncover your personal truth. Said tool happens to be the product of the two of the deepest social thinkers of the 1990's...

(turn page)

---

9 http://www.bloomberg.com/bw/articles/2013-04-18/more-mba-grads-are-switching-careers-as-job-market-improves

10 If you use the phrases "true calling," "dream job" or "professional destiny" in your application essay, you deserve whatever dumpy school accepts you.

Enter pubescent philosophers and teenage business gurus, Beavis and Butthead.

Stars of the MTV animated series that was created by Mike Judge (the guy who also created *Office Space* and *Silicon Valley* as well as *King of the Hill*), Beavis and Butthead were ne'er-do-wells who had a beautifully simple way of looking at the world—through a binary lens that divided all things into two categories: things that suck, and things that are cool.

Whether they intended to do so or not, they invented their own proprietary framework, **The Beavis and Butthead 1x2 Matrix:**

Things That Suck ⟷ Things That Are Cool

Here's how they (unintentionally) leveraged the tool to catalog their own interests:

Things That Suck ⟷	Things That Are Cool
• School	• AC/DC
• Thinking	• Nachos
• Work	• Boobs

Some might criticize this tool as being "blunt" and "lacking in nuance." And I might call these critics "butt-munching fart-knockers."

For what others see as polarity, I see as clarity. Let Maslow drone on about his hierarchy of human needs, Beavis and Butthead knew that the road to self-actualization is paved with nachos and boobs.

If you want similar clarity in your own career, start by laying out what you think is cool and what you think sucks. Acknowledging your values like this will lead you away from careers (and co-workers, companies and customers) that suck to a career (and co-workers, companies and customers) that kicks so much ass.

It works for any type of person. Let's take a look…

INTROVERTS

THINGS THAT SUCK ⟷	THINGS THAT ARE COOL
• Loud people	• Headphones
• Public speaking	• Personal space
• Human interaction	• *Dungeons & Dragons*

EXTROVERTS

THINGS THAT SUCK ←———→ THINGS THAT ARE COOL

- Silence
- Studying
- Anonymity

- Parties
- Mirrors
- Hearing selves talk

REPUBLICANS

THINGS THAT SUCK ←———→ THINGS THAT ARE COOL

- Taxes
- Regulation
- Gay marriage

- Gun
- God
- Boobs

DEMOCRATS

THINGS THAT SUCK ←———→ THINGS THAT ARE COOL

- Poverty
- Rich people
- Work

- Affordable healthcare
- Unions
- Redistributing income

As you can see, this matrix creates a very useful starting point for declaring one's values.

Here is how I cataloged work activities to decide on my eventual career choice of digital media (before I threw it all in the toilet to become a comedian/writer).

PAUL OLLINGER

THINGS THAT SUCK ⟷ THINGS THAT ARE COOL

- Paperwork
- Bureacracy
- Company politics

- Eating & drinking
- Bullshitting w/ friends
- Playing golf

Okay, so we've got something to work with here. The B&B 1x2 demonstrates that I clearly enjoyed the social side of life/business more than the...shall we say, *substantive side.*

That's a good insight!

But to understand how I could create a career out of these seemingly unemployable activities, I had to cross-reference them with jobs that would pay me to do the stuff that I like.

So, to the 1x2 Matrix, I added a *y*-axis reflecting remunerative occupations, and thus completed **The Beavis and Butthead 2x2 Career Matrix**.

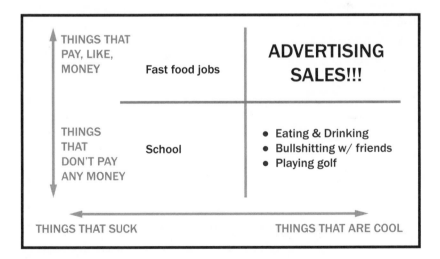

And that is how I decided to take my first post-business school job in advertising sales at the music website LAUNCH.com (that and the fact that they were the only ones who would hire me).

Applying the Framework

In many cases, the 1x2 Matrix is sufficient to understand your career calling, as in the cases below:

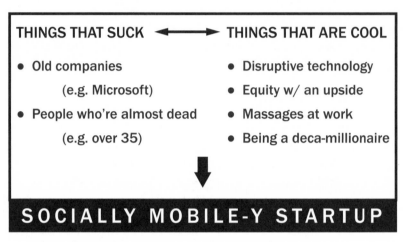

Okay, that was interesting. Let's try another one.

Maybe just one more…

THINGS THAT SUCK ⟷	THINGS THAT ARE COOL
• Dealing w/ the little people	• Making lots of money
• Creating real value	• Making lots of money
• Ethical nuance	• Making lots of money
	• Making lots of money
	• Making lots of money

INVESTMENT BANKING

Wait—just one more (I promise this time)…

THINGS THAT SUCK ⟷	THINGS THAT ARE COOL
• People who didn't go to HBS	• Taking good notes
• Not earning a commission	• Pretending you're better
• Tasteful clothing	than the sales guys
	• Saying "partnership" a lot

BUSINESS DEVELOPMENT

On the next page you'll find several blank 1x2 Matrixes for you to practice on. Cut them out, fill them out, then find out what job is right for you!

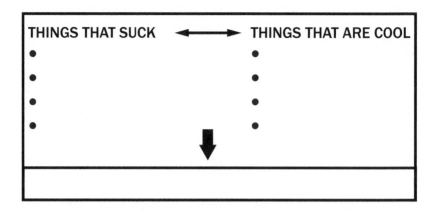

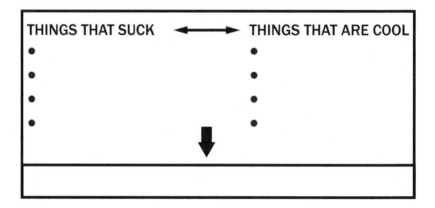

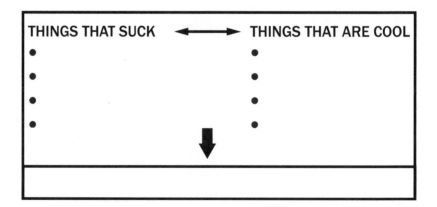

DOES GOING TO B-SCHOOL MAKE YOU AN A-HOLE?

Hollywood loves to lampoon business people. From *Wall Street's* Gordon Gekko to Michael Scott on *The Office*, the creators of TV and film often portray business people as crooks, buffoons and, most specifically, a-holes. Of course the truth differs significantly from these convenient stereotypes.

Indeed there are MBAs who are complete assholes. No doubt about it. But these cheats, money-grubbers and guys who still wear suspenders represent only a small % of the entire MBA population. Further, the general a-hole population is massive, and MBAs represent only a tiny portion thereof (see graph).

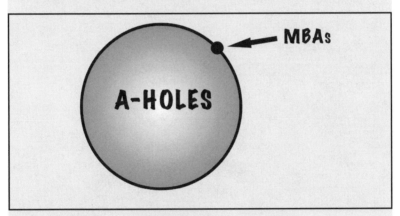

Let's zoom in a bit further to see what we're looking at here...

While some MBAs are a-holes, MBAs hardly have a monopoly on the very large population of global a-holedom.

There are far more new MBAs minted every year than there are new lawyers (source: *Slate* and *Fortune*), but the reason it doesn't feel that way is because the legal field has a much higher % Composition of Assholes (CoA).

Other observations:

- There are assholes in every profession.
- All politicians (many of whom are lawyers) are a-holes (source: people with eyes and ears).
- Some a-holes have won 21 Grammys.

When you see an MBA being an a-hole, it's often for things like insider trading or tax evasion. These are things that anyone can do, but MBAs are more likely to do them due to their predisposition to work in the financial industry.

A-HOLES

But the majority of MBA assholes are assholes for non-financial behavior. They're just everyday assholes who yell at their assistants, talk too loud on their cell phones in public and generally put their interests ahead of everyone else's.

There are also plenty of assholes in other professions:

PROFESSION	% COMPOSITION OF ASSHOLES (COA)
MBAs	16%
Lawyers	32%
Politicians	99%
MBA "comedians"	100%

Little known fact: 21% of firefighters are assholes (source: ludicrous assertion I contrived to make a point).

Oh sure, they run into burning buildings to help save other people, but the whole "getting laid whenever we want" attitude really works against them after a while.

Net: being an asshole is a choice. Decide to not be an asshole and you'll be fine.

CHAPTER 5

DOES AN MBA
PAY OFF?

M E: Hell yes it pays off.

You: Is that a guarantee?

Me: Yeah, man. Haven't you been paying attention?

You: So it will absolutely, positively have a positive financial ROI?

Me: Well…

While attaining an MBA will move you down the road to enlightenment, getting an MBA is still really, really expensive. You might logically ask yourself, "What's the ROI on enlightenment?"

Excellent question! Now you're thinking like an MBA.

Let's do the math. For our purposes here, we'll assume that you are going to HBS (hey, you deserve it).

Investment:
- HBS first year tuition for Class of 2017 = $61,225
- HBS books, materials, fees = $7,655
- Total for first year = $68,880[11]

We will assume that tuition and fees increase 5% for year two, so that:
- Total tuition and fees for second year = $72,324
- Two year total = $141,204

---

11 This does not include room, board and health insurance because you would have to pay for these whether or not you went to HBS.

Yikes! That's a lot of dough. And like the guy selling knives on late night TV says, "But wait—there's more!"

The average HBS grad walks out with about $84,000 in student debt,[12] and that debt costs money. The price is the interest that you pay until you pay it off. If you have the means, you can pay it off more quickly, but let's assume it takes you a decade to knock it all out:

- Student loan interest: 6% * $84,000 * 10 yrs = approx. $27,908
- $141k in tuition/fees + $28k in interest = $169,000

And we're still not done. Because you won't be working during your two years at HBS you have to factor in your lost wages in the calculation. Let's say you make $85,000/year at your good pre-MBA job.

Including your foregone income of $170,000, the total cost of getting a Harvard MBA (or one similar) is *about* $339,000.[13]

Holy crap. Enlightenment is expensive! Is it really worth $339,000?

Enlightenment is hard to put an exact number on, but wage growth isn't. And this is where HBS has a dynamite return *on average* (we'll get back to the assumptions we're making a little later).

If you go to HBS, you will not only get a bunch of crazy smart friends and a closet full of crimson hoodies, you'll also get *on average* a very juicy pay bump and an accelerated career path. Here's what that might look like:

Return:
- Base pay bump from $85,000 to $140,000
- Signing bonus: $25,000
- Summer internship income: $20,000
- Career accelerator (4% raises v. 2% raises)

---

12   https://www.sofi.com/mba-rankings/
13   Your personal analysis should be done net of taxes, which I am omitting here for sake of simplicity.

Let's take a look at what that pay bump and career accelerator look like in action. In the graph below, you can see that your MBA begins paying off in the form of increased income in your first year out of school. You make $55,000 more than you would have without it, and life is good.

But wait—there's more!

Because HBS has put you on an accelerated career path (and the steeper income growth trajectory that comes with it), your pay grows at a faster rate than it would have *sans*-MBA.[14] So that annual pay differential continues growing as you relish your MBA-ness and continue to kick business world ass.

It is in this stream of MBA-powered increased income that we answer the question, "Does an MBA pay off?" You can see that over your first 10 years out of HBS, your income will be $750k more than it would have been had you never pursued that MBA.

Using our friend NPV (see "Net Present Value" and "WACC" in glossary below), we then measure how much that stream of income is worth today, relative to the $369k that the MBA costs. While the NPV is less than the $750k, and varies depending on your weighted average cost of capital, in both scenarios, an HBS MBA is a homerun, positive ROI *fiesta de dinero*!

By the way, weighted average cost-of-capital is one of those great things you'll learn about at business school.

---

14 Who needs INSEAD when you can throw French around like that?

	ANNUAL INCOME W/HBS MBA (ENLIGHTENMENT)	ANNUAL IN-COME AS A SAD, NON-MBA PERSON	
ANNUAL PAY INCREASE			
YEAR	4%	2%	Δ
1	$140,000	$85,000	$55,000
2	$145,600	$86,700	$58,900
3	$151,424	$88,434	$62,990
4	$157,481	$90,203	$67,278
5	$163,780	$92,007	$71,773
6	$170,331	$93,847	$76,485
7	$177,145	$95,724	$81,421
8	$184,230	$97,638	$86,592
9	$191,600	$99,591	$92,009
10	$199,264	$101,583	$97,681
			$750,129
WACC	0.01	0.08	
NPV	$706,793	$483,488	
MBA Cost	$369,000	$369,000	
Δ	$337,793	$114,488	PARTY!!!

(I've omitted the signing bonus and internship income here
to make the graph a little cleaner)

And this is just for the first 10 years out of HBS. You will likely work for another decade or two beyond this, and in those prime earning years, that pay differential will—theoretically—be even more pronounced.

ON THE OTHER HAND…

There are some really meaningful and impactful assumptions we're making in the model above. And, to paraphrase the monetary philosopher Ol' Dirty Bastard, assumptions'll "bust yer ass." So we should be aware of them, lest our assuming asses get busted.

First, remember that the average first year income for HBS alumni includes very non-average people making *crazy* money in consulting, investment banking, hedge funds and the like. If you are not committed to a career in one of these fields (or if you're in these fields but below the mean earners in those fields), your income will likely be lower-to-much-lower. This doesn't mean that your HBS degree will have a negative ROI over the long run, but it just might take longer to break even. That's worth keeping in mind.

Second, these reported incomes are skewed way high by alumni living in New York, London, San Francisco and Hong Kong, i.e. the most expensive cities in the world. So while they may be making hundreds of thousands of dollars a year, they may also be paying $4,000/month (or lots more) to rent a one-bedroom apartment. You shouldn't look at these average incomes and think, "I am going to live like a king on $175,000/year in Tulsa, OK!" 'Cuz that's probably not where you're going to find these juicy pay packages.

Third, you are a growing and evolving human being. Your interests, desires and passions will change over time. The career you find intriguing right out of business school might not float your boat 5, 10 or 15 years later. Maybe you just decide that you're not interested in doing [FILL IN THE NAME OF CAREER] any more, and that you really want to [WORK WITH KIDS / DO SOMETHING FOR THE DEVELOPING WORLD / BECOME A STAND-UP COMEDIAN]. Or maybe the grind of an 80+ hour work week is something you can tolerate when you're young and single but not when you're older, married and raising children. Or maybe some health issues present themselves and you need to hit "pause" on your career to deal with them. In any of these scenarios, the juicy comp packages and steepened earning curves pretty much fly out the window.

Fourth, the model above represents an uninterrupted, positive career trajectory. Due to the vicissitudes of the market, the economy and personal wackness, careers often do not maintain a smooth progression upward and to the right.

If historical economic trends continue, you should expect some kind of ugly macroeconomic tornado to blow through every seven years or so. Whether it's dot-com bubbles busting, global mortgages imploding or Adam Smith's invisible hand getting caught in the cookie jar, bad stuff that is way out of your control happens, and it's going to affect your career.

So imagine the scenario in Graph 2 below. You get out of school and everything goes dandy for two years. Then in year three, the world explodes and you get fired/laid-off/made redundant from your job. Maybe you saw it coming or maybe you didn't, but that doesn't really matter as you getting canned is the result of an industry-wide meltdown and no one—I mean *no one*—in your industry is hiring.

So you sit on the sidelines for a whole year and log a goose-egg in the old income column. Meanwhile, you still got those big ol' student loans hanging over your head, with the interest meter still running.

	ANNUAL INCOME W/ HBS MBA (ENLIGHT-ENMENT)	ANNUAL INCOME AS A SAD, NON-MBA PERSON	
	ANNUAL PAY INCREASE		
YEAR	4%	2%	Δ
1	$140,000	$85,000	$55,000
2	$145,600	$86,700	$58,900
3	$32,855	$88,434	-$55,579
4	$117*	$90,203	-$90,086
5	$84,220**	$92,007	-$7,787
6	$102,314	$93,847	$8,467
7	$104,360	$95,724	$8,636
8	$108,535	$97,638	$10,896
9	$112,876	$99,591	$13,285
10	$117,391	$101,583	$15,808
			$17,542
WACC	0.01	0.08	
NPV	$16,824	$16,018	
MBA Cost	$369,000	$369,000	
Δ	-$352,176	-$352,982	*NO PARTY!!!*

*Oh no, recession hits!
**New job.
(Even if you throw the signing bonus and
internship income back in, this sucks)

At least one person has gone to the trouble to write a book about this significant potential downside of paying for and/or financing an expensive MBA. In her 2013 book, *The MBA Bubble*, Mariana Zenetti lays out the argument that MBA programs around the world are over-priced, over-hyped and selling naïve students a degree they don't need.

She makes the point that investing in an expensive MBA in Spain (where she went to school) would have been a bad idea— just as buying an over-priced house during the Spanish real estate bubble was a bad idea—right before the world plunged into the Great Recession and Spain experienced unemployment rates over 26%.[15]

Well…yeah.

An MBA isn't a Harry Potter invisibility cloak that hides you from nuclear macroeconomic meltdown. It also won't give you x-ray vision or the ability to fly.

Further, some people just aren't down for the whole business school experience itself. The long hours, grueling workload and late night stress-busting parties don't suit everyone's lifestyle.

So while I disagree with her premise and am bullish as all hell on what the MBA did for me, she brings up a point worth including here: *for some people, the MBA will not pay off financially.*

Prospective business school students should do their due diligence to make sure they know what they are getting into. Some MBA programs saddle their graduates with massive piles of debt without providing an income that enables the graduate to battle that debt monster.[16] A degree from a school ranked #50 might provide you with a leg up, but it will not do the same thing for a career that a degree from Wharton or Kellogg would.

Even from the top schools, an MBA is a powerful credential, but it is only potential financial energy until you turn it into debt-slashing income through year after year of hard work.

---

15   http://www.tradingeconomics.com/spain/unemployment-rate
16   https://www.sofi.com/mba-rankings/

Net: don't pursue business school unless you can pay for it outright or you're committed to paying back your loans. Enter the process with eyes wide open—these loans are big numbers that grow while you sleep. Their very existence will exacerbate the stress of any fluctuations in your career. Banishing them from your post-grad life might mean sticking with a job you don't love for a lot longer than you otherwise would have…assuming that's even within your control.

OTHER THINGS YOU CAN BUY WITH $141,000

Two years of tuition at HBS will cost you about $141,000. Even if you have this kind of cash sitting in your sock drawer next to your weed, it's worth evaluating how it could best be put to use. So before you decide to blow all that dough on a world-class MBA, consider some of these alternative investments.

2015 Porsche 911 GT3

Car and Driver calls the GT3 "a rolling deity." With 475 HP, the GT3 goes from 0 to 60 MPH in a mind-blowing 3.0 seconds. It won't teach you how to price a bond, but think of the time you'll save getting to and from the grocery store. Oh man this car is bad ass. It'll look amazing parked outside your place next to your roommate's used Camry.

Private Jet Tour Around the World

For 24 days on the Four Seasons round-the-world global jet tour, you will travel like you're already a rich MBA on a tricked-out private 757. You will avoid security lines and the hoi polloi while the pampering crew stuffs your face with warm nuts, shellfish and culture, pickling you with champagne served intravenously.

When it's over, you won't have a monetizable career credential, but you'll have amazing memories, great Facebook photos and one hell of a case of the gout.

By the way, $140k only pays for you and some incidentals. If you want to take a date, plan on almost double this amount. Good news being that he/she will definitely be impressed and you will totally get lucky.

A 3 bedroom, 2 bath home in Grove City, OH

Maybe this doesn't sound super exciting. But what if I told you that Grove City is the hometown of Richard Cordray? What do you mean you've never heard of him? He's the very first Director of the federal government's new Consumer Financial Protection Bureau, i.e. he's the guy making sure you don't get screwed over by unscrupulous student loan providers. Geesh, do your homework. Anyway, owning a cute little home in Ohio isn't going to make you rich, but it would certainly be a step toward stability and security…which is just what Richard wants for you.

A private concert by Carly Rae Jepsen[17]

Hey, I just met you, and this is crazy, but here's a concert to impress the ladies! (Or dudes.) Unlike your business school

17   Source: Celebrity Talent International

tuition, government-subsidized loans are not available to help finance this event, but you shouldn't write off the value of having CRJ headline a party at your crib. It may not increase your long-term income, but you will be the most popular kid in your dorm for a few days at least.

12,744 cases of Zico chocolate-flavored coconut water

Admittedly, it does sound like a lot of coconut water, but this stuff is hella delicious, and it'll keep you mad-hydrated for years, dawg. (Shipping not included.)

17,647 Bloomin' Onions at Outback Steakhouse

You don't need more than one Bloomin' Onion to experience the concept of declining marginal returns, but with over 17,000, you'll never forget. At 1,954 calories each, you also get over 34 million calories to use as you see fit. Come to think of it, buy the Porsche.

CHAPTER 6

WHY ARE PEOPLE TALKING SMACK ABOUT MBAs?

IF YOU'VE STARTED YOUR RESEARCH INTO TOP MBA programs, you have no doubt run across plenty of naysaying voices in the blogosphere / internetosphere arguing that business school is a waste of time and money. MBA bashing is at an all time high.

Okay, I don't have any real data to base that claim on, but let's just say that there are a whole bunch of high profile people out there saying that business school doesn't matter. It's gotten so popular to do so that those claiming to be challenging the status quo (that an MBA is an antiquated tool for corporate success) are really just parroting the fashionable ("Meh-BA") attitude.

Recent headlines include the following:

- 10 Reasons You Don't Need an MBA (*Forbes*)

- Why Spending $150k On An MBA Is Probably A Dumb Idea (*Forbes*)

- An MBA is a complete waste of time and money for anyone who wants to create or join a startup (*Boston.com* in an article by David Cancel, Chief Product Officer at Hubspot)

- I Quickly Learned Why Silicon Valley Loves to Hate MBAs (*BusinessInsider*)

The bashing is particularly rough in Silicon Valley, where leading venture capitalists and executives insist that business school doesn't help—and very well might hurt—one's professional advancement.

In a recent Quora post ("Is getting an MBA worth it?") that was viewed almost one million times, a very senior and well-respected venture capitalist wrote "most elite business schools teach directionally wrong advice," and concluded that MBAs programs "adversely attract people who value credentials."

(Okay, he got me on that last one.)

Consider also the words of Marc Andreesen, the venture capitalist and Silicon Valley legend who, as the co-author of Mosaic, brought the internet to the masses in the 1990s:

> *"MBA graduating classes are actually a reliable contrary indicator: if they all want to go into investment banking, there's going to be a financial crisis. If they want to go into tech, that means a bubble is forming."*

Well, I never!

As an MBA and digital media veteran who had a great career in tech, I'm not going to just sit here and let these people defame the beloved degree that keeps my self-esteem warm at night.

So, I hereby go on record as taking great exception to this bashing for three important reasons:

1. I wouldn't write a whole book about a degree that was useless. (Would I?)
2. Contrived outrage is good for publicity.

And, most importantly...

3. If these people are right, then my entire professional self-concept is a wretched, hollow fantasy.

But more than just being pretend outraged, I'm surprised that the chorus of MBA-bashers in technology remains so strong when the data tells a very different story.

So what is going on here?

LET'S THINK LIKE TECHNOLOGISTS

In developing and scaling its amazing portfolio of products, Facebook and many other top tech companies religiously follow some version of the this mantra:

- Observe what people (users) do.
- Ignore what they say they do.

That same perspective should be kept in mind when reading these kinds of comments about the value of MBAs in Silicon Valley.

While senior tech executives and investors are saying that the MBA doesn't matter, what the industry is doing tells a very different story. And what they're doing is hiring and promoting a whole bunch of MBAs.

Indeed, when you look under the hood, it becomes clear that top technology companies are falling all over themselves to attract new business school graduates, and that the MBAs who are already in the industry are kicking prodigious amounts of ass.

Take Amazon for example. The *Financial Times* reported last year that the dominant retailer expected to hire hundreds of MBAs in 2015. These grads will work in operations, finance, product management and consumer leadership, according to the company's director of University Services, Miriam Park, who happens to be a graduate of MIT's Sloan School of Management.[18]

Amazon is hiring these MBAs aggressively for positions in the U.S., China, Japan and Europe where they recruit from London Business School, Insead, Iese, Esade IMD and Oxford Saïd.

Back here in the States, they cast their net beyond the usual suspects like HBS, Stanford and Kellogg. This year the retailing giant hired 12 graduates from Vanderbilt's Owen School and a record 59 of the 455 MBA graduates of Michigan's Class of 2015. Joining them in Ross' top 10 hiring companies were Microsoft at #6 and Dell at #10.

At MIT Sloan, Amazon, Google, Apple and Microsoft were among the top eight employers of MBA grads, with Amazon hiring 22 Sloanies, the second biggest hirer at the school behind only McKinsey & Co.

Similar scenarios are taking place at pretty much all top business schools. At UCLA's Anderson, Google, Amazon and Microsoft each hired more than 10 new grads last year, with Adobe, Apple, Ebay, Samsung, Symantec and VMWare hiring at least 5 each.

---

18   Though as an MSc, Management, not an MBA.

So clearly tech companies are hiring all the new MBAs they can. As strong as these numbers are, they don't include the large number of b-school graduates who will end up in technology after working in banking or consulting for a few years.

So what if you are two or three years out of your MBA program and looking for a job in Silicon Valley? Is there demand out there for your services?

To answer this question, I put myself in the role of MBA job-seeker. I went to Microsoft's jobs listing page (http://Careers. Microsoft.com) and typed into their search box "MBA preferred" (in quotes so that "MBA preferred" has to appear in the listing). The search provided 170 jobs.

Not bad, but what about the broader job market for MBAs in the technology business?

Good question. For that answer, I used career site Indeed.com's advanced search tool. I set location to within 50 miles of "Silicon Valley, CA," typed in "MBA preferred," and was greeted by 1,024 potential jobs.

That's a lot of jobs, but they're probably all just in finance, right? Wrong.

It seems top tech companies are looking for MBAs to help them in all kinds of positions, including:

- Product management
- Project management
- Business development
- Business planning
- Warehouse management
- Supply chain management
- Demand generation
- Strategic alliances
- Strategy
- Accounting
- Finance
- Marketing
- Social media
- Operations
- Sales
- Sales analytics
- Compliance
- Advertising
- Public relations
- And many, many more

And these jobs were not just at a few good companies—but at a plethora of great companies. Including, but not limited to (at a certain point I just quit counting):

- Tesla
- Uber
- PayPal
- Google
- Apple
- Hewlett-Packard
- Tivo
- Genentec
- Symantec
- Facebook
- esurance
- Flextronics
- Walmart ecommerce
- Veritas Technologies
- Move, Inc.
- Cisco
- VMware
- LegalZoom
- Intuit
- Salesforce
- Samsung
- Mastercard
- Thermo Fisher Scientific
- Intel
- Minted
- Stitch Fix
- Fitbit
- ADARA Networks
- Sony Electronics
- Stella & Dot
- Allergan
- Mckesson
- Calsoft Labs
- OpenX
- Amazon
- NTT Data
- Roche
- Honeywell
- Oracle
- SAP
- Abbott Labs
- Electronic Arts
- Avaya
- Philips
- Verizon
- Ancestry
- Fidelity
- Levi Strauss
- Lifelock
- Adobe

(To say nothing of the excellent opportunities at Jamba Juice.)

These results clearly demonstrated the strong demand for MBAs in the tech industry so I decided to take it one step further: I went to LinkedIn to get a feel for how many MBAs were already working in Silicon Valley.

Of course LinkedIn profile information is self-reported by the user and may not be current. However, it's pretty solid directional data.

Here are a few interesting nuggets related to the prevalence of just Harvard Business School alums working at leading tech firms:

- LinkedIn itself employs about 60 HBS grads, eBay employs 31 and PayPal employs 22.

These—and other—MBAs are not just the rank-and-file either.

Check this out: according to LinkedIn, 17 of 48 Facebook executives (VP+) hold MBAs. That's 35% of the executive team! (I learned how to do math like that in business school.) So while an MBA might not be necessary to get a job at the social media giant, it sure as hell isn't going to hurt your chances of advancing once you're in the door.

So why do they bash?

It puzzles me why so many important people in Silicon Valley would say that MBAs don't matter when it is quite clear that they do. Maybe it's just the prevailing ethos and to say otherwise would be impolitic.

Perhaps the stereotypical extroverted, loudmouth MBA personality fits poorly with the more introverted engineers who run a lot of technology companies. Could it be that a few cocky, know-it-all bad apples have been so catastrophically self-absorbed (oh Lord I hope I wasn't one of them) that they have just ruined the rap for the rest of us?

Whatever the reason behind this label, it's one that new MBAs need to keep in mind. Fair or unfair, many of your new post-business school colleagues will expect you to fit into their long-held MBA perceptions.

The good news is that this affords you the opportunity to surprise them not just with your brilliance, but also with your humility, thoughtfulness and interest in their opinion. Having others say or think things like "Wow—she's an MBA, but she really listens!" is a great way to establish your personal brand.

It matters because this is an industry that is dying for your help! And while one certainly doesn't need an MBA to be an entrepreneur, entrepreneurs need lots of MBAs to scale their companies and operate them efficiently as they grow.

Net: it's a great time to be an MBA in Silicon Valley. Even if very few tech leaders will say so.

CHAPTER 7

WHAT'S SCHOOL LIKE?

THERE ARE AS MANY OPINIONS ON THE BUSINESS SCHOOL experience as there are business school students and alumni. To some it is a grueling academic ultra-marathon. To others, it is a two-year vacation with an open bar.

I found school to be both exhilarating and exhausting, the hardest but most rewarding two years of my life up to that point. First year was especially brutal. They threw heaping volumes of work at us, seemingly just to see what we could handle. We could not possibly complete it all. These anaerobic academics forced us to prioritize which tasks we would finish, and which we would have to leave well short of perfection.

Some programs are harder than others. Some students take it more seriously than others. I took it relatively seriously if only because I wanted to prove that I could hold my own in that amazing group of students…or at least not be a complete waste of space.

Academic Life: The Core and Grades

To be an MBA, you should have some minimal competence with the main topics of the business world and the written and spoken fluency to express yourself in a clear and persuasive manner. At most schools, students must complete a "core" set of classes that include some mix of the following:
- Marketing
- Corporate Finance
- Accounting
- Data/Decisions Analysis
- Operations
- Managerial Economics
- Statistics

- Leadership/Organization Behavior
- Management Communications
- Ethics class[19]

Some schools include more classes in the core, some fewer, but that list represents the most common classes that all students must complete. The future marketers must understand the basics of finance. The future bankers must demonstrate some understanding of marketing. While some of the hardcore finance types in your class will scoff at the "softer" Communications stuff, it's one of the few classes you will use every single day in your post-MBA career. It is also one of the areas in which many (many!) younger professionals need help because they produce PowerPoint presentations that look like Escher paintings and write e-mails that read like drunken fraternity newsletters.

After completing your school's core, you will have the opportunity to dive into the electives of your choice. At many schools, you will be able to take courses outside of the business school, occasionally with undergrads.

Academic Life: Grades

Grading systems differ from school to school. Some schools (e.g. Wharton, Booth, Stern, Kellogg) use the A-B-C-D-F grading system. HBS uses a three-tier category with a forced curve and a cap on allowable grades of "Tier 3" (i.e. "you pass, but you suck"). There's also the very rare Tier 4 which means "just go away, idiot."

Many of the other top schools utilize a system that looks something like this:

- **H—Honors**: awarded to a small % of the class. I never saw any evidence of this grade. As far as I'm concerned, it doesn't exist.

---

19 Thrown in by the school so that when one of their alums gets busted doing something sketchy post-graduation, the school can say, "Hey, we told her not to do it!"

- **High pass or S+:** It means, "You're okay, kid. But don't get too cocky."

- **P or S—Pass or Satisfactory**: The grade that most students get. You are making decent progress toward being an MBA.

- **LP—Low Pass**: Also known as a "loop," as in, "Thank God I looped that class. I thought I was going to fail!" or "Can you believe Professor So-and-So looped 20% of the class? Not cool!"

- **F—Fail**: Also stands for "Fast food industry," which is where you'll be working if you get more than one of these.

Competition for grades in business school ranges from the not-so-serious to *Hunger Games / Lord of the Flies*—throat-slashing Darwinism. Some schools force a curve a bit harder than others, either encouraging this behavior or exacerbating its students' natural survivalist tendencies.

Grades are basically as important as you want them to be. Not one person has asked me about my business school grades since I graduated. Not one prospective employer. Not one prospective spouse.

Perhaps the answer ("me grades not so goodish") was written all over my slack-jawed face. More likely, it's that they just don't matter as much in business school (see caveat below). The fact that I had finagled my way into and through a top program was a good enough signal of brains and ambition. Beyond that, employers and spouses are just looking for the right fit and a full head of hair (a class I failed).

I don't even know where I finished in my class, but I assume it was cozily in the bottom 50%, and it hasn't mattered. In my chosen corporate career (digital media sales), having an MBA (and a good one at that) is such an anomaly that people probably think,

"Boy to have that degree and still end up in this career, you must have screwed up good and proper."

Where it does matter is in the pursuit of a job with the super-elite employers like Goldman Sachs, McKinsey and Google. Some schools (e.g., Harvard, Stanford) deny employers access to grades, but you just know those devious smarty-pantses who went into these careers have other ways of signaling superiority over their classmates (e.g. telling the recruiter "Don't hire Dave—he's a moron").

Some people are driven to get the best grades, period. I was less concerned with the grades themselves than I was with making sure I carried my weight in study group as best as I could, and that I didn't look completely stupid when the dreaded cold calls came my way (I achieved less than 100% success in this endeavor).

Net: it's not your grades that matter so much in business school—it is *your brand* in the minds of your classmates, professors and, indeed, yourself. I didn't need to be thought of as the smartest guy in the class, but I didn't want to be seen as a knucklehead either. I guess what I really wanted was for others to feel that I deserved my spot in a class full of very accomplished people.

Academic Life: Study Groups

Much of the academic work at business school happens in study groups of four to six students who band together (either voluntarily or not) to complete their homework (yes, "homework" sounds like grade school, but that's what it is).

This group construct is supposed to simulate life in the corporate world and helps promote teamwork. Whether that's true or not, it definitely forces study group members to complete assignments without choking the living crap out of each other.

Study groups can be amazing and the foundation for life-long friendships. Or, they can be not so great. As a few alumni put it:

"It started out great [but then] one of the members went nuts when the work load increased. It was a disaster."

Here are a few tips for study group survival and etiquette:

1. **Choose study group members who complement your skillset:** If you're not on the smart end of the study group spectrum, hitch yourself to a fast team of horses, and try to hold on. If you're smart, pick a group who can help you improve your speaking skills or teach you how to pick out a tie. Note: at many schools, study groups are not your choice so much as they are thrust upon you. Good luck with that.

2. **Know your role:** The world needs coffee-fetchers and someone to change the printer paper (this was my area of expertise). See "Comparative Advantage."

3. **Keep it in your pants:** Intra-study group dating is not recommended, but it happens. Hormones do not help one focus, and sex with a smart, gorgeous classmate is way more fun than Statistics or Operations 201. But know that business school is generally a cozy environment and few secrets make it all the way to graduation.

Look out for These Study Group Personalities:

- **The Asshole:** This guy acts as if your group assignment is all that stands between the present and him being promoted to CEO. While the ambition is admirable, he is a major earth-scorcher and #1 candidate in your class to be jailed for insider trading.

- **The Moron:** How in the hell did this idiot make it past the admissions committee? His presence will make you doubt the rigor of the selection process that damn near killed you. You'll eventually piece together that his dad is

97

some big-check-writing muckety-muck friend of a board member (which is great for the school, but doesn't do much for you getting your cases done before midnight).

- **The Crier:** Major stress case who cracks under the pressure of workload, competition and cat-management distractions. Derails study group for 30 minutes at a time as everyone looks at their shoes, excuses themselves to the rest room or otherwise tries not to tell them to shut the hell up. Becomes the job of The Asshole to pull a General Patton and slap Crier back to reality.

- **Rocket Man/Woman:** Quant jock with undergrad from MIT, Carnegie-Mellon or Georgia Tech. No ego other than expecting you to know he/she is a genius and way smarter than you. Recognize this and this person is your best pal. You can help them a little bit with basic pre-interview fashion tips like "you might want to tie your shoes." You need this person.

- **Sex Kitten:** Rocket Man/Woman hates her/secretly desires her. If nothing else, her presence means everyone in study group adheres to certain minimum levels of personal hygiene.

- **The Mascot/Comic Relief:** Provides levity more than substance. He's worth having around because he makes things fun, but manage your expectations of what he's going to contribute to the team academically (see above note about getting coffee and changing printer paper). If your study group was a rock band, he's the charming but relatively talent-less guy who plays the tambourine.

- **The Wack Job:** Smart enough person, but makes everyone wonder, "Who is this freak-show?" Be amazed as he tops his last non sequitur with an even more bizarre conclusion about a set of data, the results of a football game or life in general. You'll hear him say things like "We used to have trains!" or "Enron was onto something…" and scream "Wait—what?!?" as you pound your head on the table in disbelief. He is never to present on behalf of the group.

- **The International Grammatical Disaster:** You must first acknowledge that it is extraordinarily difficult to come to a new country and communicate in a foreign tongue at a high level of fluency. Also that many who learned English as a second language often speak more correctly than native speakers. But once-in-a-blue-moon, in a moment of semi-xenophobic weakness, you will find yourself looking at one of the international students in your class and channeling Jules Winnfield from *Pulp Fiction* who fumed: "English, motherfucker! Do you speak it?"

- **The Free Rider:** Defined thusly by Wikipedia—"those who benefit from resources, goods or services but do not pay for them," The Free Rider thrives in study groups wherein not all participate in the work, yet all receive the same grade. Real world examples of free riders include career politicians, all the members of *NSYNC who aren't named "Justin Timberlake" and all the European Union countries not named "Germany."

While we're talking about what you'll encounter on any business school campus, let's dive into the language of the MBA, who speaks in her own code.

MBA-TALK GLOSSARY

2x2 Matrix: A dual-axis chart on which to plot attributes of things (products, businesses, prospective lovers) using two continua of opposing characteristics like size (large / small) and cost (cheap / expensive), creating four quadrants. Put another way, it's a big ass square with lines through the middle of it. By tradition, the top right quadrant is where the desirable things land. All other quadrants are for losers.

3 C's: Business model developed by Kenichi Ohmae. Customer, Competitors, Corporation that lead to strategic advantage. It analyzes how the dynamics of Customer, Competition, and Corporation lead to strategic advantage (see—three C's!).

4 P's of Marketing: Four things—Product, Place, Price, Promotion—contribute to make a product successful or not. The 4 P's have nothing to do with "OPP."

Amortization: Depreciation's cousin (ask one of the accountants in your class to explain the difference). Also "The Spanish art of love." When you add "amor" to something, you have "amortized" it.

Accounts Payable: Stuff you owe other people.

Accounts Receivable: Stuff other people owe you.

Annual Report: A "year in review" holiday letter written for the amusement of Wall Street analysts who cover your company. It is cheery even when things are not.

Annuity: A stream of payments someone owes you. Very useful concept if you are a bookie.

Appreciation: When assets increase in value—and what I'd like to get a little more of in my life. Damn.

Arbitrage: When you buy and sell something at the same time, exploiting market inefficiencies (by which I mean "inside information").

At the end of the day: A stupid term used by people who like to hear themselves talk. It means "when the deal is over" but that is way too mundane for the cool kids who drop this dope lingo. Don't say it.

Balance Sheet: It's how much stuff you got (assets) on one side and how much you owe (liabilities) on the other. Hopefully it balances.

Best Practice: As Montell Jordan would say, "This is how we do *iiiit*… (This is how we do it.)"

Black-Scholes Formula: A (you guessed it) formula to estimate the value of an option. It's like the quadratic equation for rich people.

Blue Ocean: A nerdy way of describing a market that has yet to be chummed up with competitors or great whites (which are, btw, man-eating killing machines).

CAGR: Compound Annual Growth Rate. The average amount of annual investment growth over a period of time. You will hear it pronounced like 'cagger' or 'kayger.' If someone pronounces it "kegel" or "cougar," they are either very dumb or very funny (or both).

Cannibalization: When a new product's sales' gains come at the expense of an existing product's sales. Or the unfortunate by-product of a poorly-timed wagon ride through the Sierra Nevada.

Caveat Emptor: Latin phrase meaning "buyer beware." Appropriate to keep in mind when making the gigantic financial commitment to pursue an MBA.

Ceteris paribus: Latin meaning "assume all that other garbage remains constant."

C-Level: Officers of a company. Traditionally the CEO, CFO, CTO and COO. Today companies have all kinds of stupid chief titles, including Chief People Person, Chief Knowledge Officer, Chief Innovation Officer and Chief Evangelist Officer. These titles mean jack squat.

Collusion: In business, the practice of working with third parties to gain an unfair market advantage. In other words, it's business.

Comparative Advantage: Economic theory stating that owners of resources are best off applying them to those tasks yielding the highest relative return. In other words, it is doing that thing at which they suck the least.

COGS: Cost of Goods Sold. The cost of the direct labor and materials that go into making a product or batch of products. Not included in COGS are the costs of the factory, marketing expenses or the well-deserved commission earned by the honest salesman without whom the product would still be sitting in the warehouse.

Decision Tree: A graphic tool that helps you realize that no matter what you do, you're likely screwed.

Delta: The difference between A and B. Also an airline whose planes tend to smell like stale farts. It looks like this Δ.

Depreciation: Amortization's cousin. It's the path your bean-counters take toward making all your assets appear worthless to the IRS.

EBITDA: Earnings before interest, taxes depreciation and amortization. So it's earnings, and then when someone tries to bring up the other stuff, the CFO puts her fingers in her ears and starts going "la-la-la-la I can't hear you asking about interest, taxes or the other stuff..."

FIFO: First In, First Out system of inventory management that my wife REFUSES to follow when it comes to the dairy products in our refrigerator. It makes me really mad.

First Mover: The party who gets to a market early and reaps the rewards and/or penalties for so doing. See the concept at work in the college party hook-up strategy known as "go ugly early."

Greater Fool Theory: If you don't know what this is, I have some great investment opportunities for you.

Gross Profit: Gross profit is the difference between the price paid for a good and the cost of goods sold (COGS). It could also be used to describe profits in dirty industries like sewage, Porta-potties and garbage collection. I mean, #Gross!

Insider Trading: The illegal use of non-public information to win huge trading profits. One of the most common ways that b-school nerds end up in the slammer.

Invisible Hand: The will of the free market, driven by aggregate consumer or supplier behavior. Also what Adam Smith used to get Mrs. Smith all excited.

IPO: Initial Public Offering. When the shares of a previously-private company are offered for sale to the public, thus creating a market for the stock and enabling early employees or investors to sell their shares and get super rich(er).

IRR: Internal Rate of Return. It's like ROI (I think).

Low Hanging Fruit: The easiest market opportunities to pursue, e.g. getting an MBA instead of a PhD in Neuroscience.

Market Penetration: I wouldn't touch this one with my invisible hand.

MECE: An acronym for a McKinsey-created data analysis concept called "Mutually exclusive, completely exhaustive."

It's pronounced "me-see," and here's how you can use it in a sentence: "Me see a consulting dork."

Net: The total of something after removing all costs or liabilities (see Net-Net).

Net-Net: This means "net" but people feel cooler when they say "net-net" for some reason. These are the same people who say "at the end of the day."

NPV: Net Present Value. The math that lottery winners need to do to evaluate the "lump sum" or annuity options (which is ironic because most lottery winners aren't very good at math).

OPM: Stands for "Other People's Money," which is a great way to fund risky operations.

OPP: Sort of like OPM, but different. OPP is not a business term (not strictly speaking anyway). How can I explain it?

Opportunity Cost: How much the cost of doing one thing costs you in foregone opportunity of doing something else. It's a concept my wife reminds me of constantly when she says, "you know, I could have married Jason Abromowitz—his podiatry practice is booming!"

Options: A financial instrument that gives you the (wait for it) option to buy or sell an underlying stock, bond or commodity at a previously established price. Options are financial crack that can make you rich or wipe you out in mere minutes. Smoke up and git you some!

Partnership: What a sales person calls it when he gets your money and gives you nothing in return save his crappy product. The only real partnerships are those in which ALL "partners" have money or a meaningful portion of their life (i.e. "sweat equity") in the game. If you lend your name or reputation to a project, you are a licensor, not a partner.

Perfect Storm: Find a port because you are effed.

Porter's 5 Forces: A framework developed by HBS professor / business guru / strategy demigod Michael Porter that outlines the degree to which a company is or is not totally screwed.

Portfolio Theory: Means don't put all your nest egg in one basket. Spread that goodness around so that when one part of the market inevitably explodes, you don't lose everything.

Profit-Maximization: Producing where marginal revenue = marginal cost. In other words, work until you squeeze the last God-forsaken penny out of your business.

Red Ocean: A nerdy way of describing a market chummed up with competitors and man-killing sharks. This term makes surfing Aussies very nervous.

ROI: Return on Investment. The % profit you made on your capital (more or less).

Signaling: See "collusion."

Stakeholder: Employees, customers, consumers, investors, vendors, neighbors, relatives, devotees, Twitter followers or anyone who has a real or imagined interest in your company.

Sunk Cost: Sunk costs are all the stupid crap you did or invested in in the past. These experiences and baggage have no bearing on decisions you make going forward. In other words, the past is an anchor—you have only your future to consider. It's kind of a beautiful concept, and most often used by those who have screwed up on a colossal level.

SWOT Analysis: Framework for analyzing a business' situation by looking at their $\underline{S}$trengths, $\underline{W}$eaknesses, $\underline{O}$pportunities, $\underline{T}$hreats. They were going to call it TOWS, but SWOT sounds a lot cooler.

Synergy: Efficiencies achieved from working with another party. One of the most abused business phrases there is.

Thinking "Out of the Box": Never mind what it's supposed to mean—just don't say it.

Unlevered Purchasing Power Parity (PPP): Something to do with the relative strength of currencies.

Utility: Economic term meaning "the good shit."

Value Proposition: Know yours before you start your business school applications.

Wall Street: A street in downtown Manhattan that is home to the New York Stock Exchange (NYSE) and a bunch of overworked people in expensive suits.

Wall Street (movie, 1986): Directed by Oliver Stone who is likely a socialist and does not appear to believe in capitalism, it nevertheless inspired multiple generations of future traders, bankers, buyout and hedge funders who now run the world while incessantly quoting Mr. Stone's words.

Weighted Average Cost of Capital: How much it costs you to get access to money, whether you borrow it or issue equity and stuff.

Win-Win: A mutually beneficial deal between two parties.

Win-Win-Win: A three-way deal wherein all parties benefit.

Win-Win-Win-Win: Now you're just being silly.

Zero Sum: A scenario (game, transaction, marriage) wherein one side winning means the other side loses. It's a hard world—toughen up.

CHAPTER 8

WHERE SHOULD
I GO?

"You may decide you want to go to Harvard or Stanford. And I would ask you 'Why?' You would reply, 'Because they're the best.' I would say, 'First of all, shut the hell up. WHY do you want to go there?' You'd go, 'I want to go there because they are the best and that's where I belong.' And I'd get kind of frustrated but resign myself to the fact that, with that attitude, you're probably right."
—Fabricated Quote, Attributable to No One

So you're convinced that the MBA is right for you, and you are committed to go getcha one. Good for you!

The next logical question is, "Which school is right for you?"

While all schools offer the MBA degree, each school offers a different set of characteristics, e.g. brand name, academic strengths, network and location. These attributes will provide most of their value in the few years after graduation, but will continue to be a part of your *curriculum vitae* for decades.

This is why you must strive for a firm understanding of how the business school experience and degree fits into your overall career and life goals. You should take these factors into account:

Industry Focus

Each top business school program has a unique set of strengths. Some are better positioned than others to launch you into a career in a chosen industry.

For example, if you want to set Wall Street on fire metaphorically-speaking, then think Wharton, Harvard or Columbia. While UC Berkeley can get you there, it's probably not your strongest bet. But if you want to set Wall Street on fire literally, then maybe it is. (Haas people, relax—I'm talking about the dirty "Occupy Wall Street" hippies down the street from you in the UC Sociology department.)

On the other hand, if you're gunning for a career in technology, Berkeley-located Haas is on the right ventricle of Silicon Valley and boasts a killer network of alumni wired through the current and future Googles, Ubers and Airbnbs. And while Stanford is probably the first choice for those looking to launch the next Facebook, Haas should be way up there in your considered set.

Geography

Speaking of the Bay Area, a school doesn't have to be adjacent to downtown Palo Alto (like Stanford) to have recruiting mojo in technology. Nor does a program have to be in New York City to wield heft on Wall Street. Every year, top programs are using their resources and creativity to combat geographical weaknesses (or— said more positively—to augment their traditional strengths).

Consider, for example, Wharton West, U Penn's west coast outpost in the middle of San Francisco. While it serves mostly as center for executive education, it also provides a semester-long home for Wharton MBA candidates seeking a real, tangible Silicon Valley connection.

Wharton financial cred + Silicon Valley exposure = a legit competitor to Stanford.

But geography affects more than just where a school has its strongest industry ties. Geography has strong implications to your day-to-day life. For example, do you get to class via the subway (Columbia and NYU), snow mobile (Chicago, Kellogg, Tuck, Cornell) or skateboard (Stanford, Berkeley, UCLA).

Clearly, geography means weather. Do you kick it in the sunshine or freeze your ass off in the woods? Would you rather stroll on the warm Stanford quad in flip-flops or trudge through the slosh on the icy sidewalks of Philadelphia? Given that the top three California schools (Stanford, UCLA and UC Berkeley) all have admit rates under 20%, there are obviously many who prefer studying in the warmer climes (those weak souls).

	US NEWS & WORLD REPORT'S TOP 10 MBA PROGRAMS RANKED BY AVERAGE TEMPERATURE IN JANUARY			
RANK	SCHOOL	USNR RANK-ING	LOCATION	AVERAGE TEMPERA-TURE IN JANUARY
1	UC Berkeley	7	Berkeley, CA	58/42
2	Stanford	1	Stanford, CA	58/38
3	UVA	10	Charlottesville, VA	45/27
4	Wharton	3	Philadelphia, PA	40/26
5	Columbia	8	New York, NY	39/26
T6	Harvard	2	Boston, MA	36/22
T6	MIT	5	Cambridge, MA	36/22
T8	Kellogg	6	Evanston, IL	32/18
T8	U Chicago	4	Chicago, IL	32/18
10	Dartmouth	9	Hanover, NH	28/10

Region also matters because it determines to some degree where you might end up living after graduation. You can certainly go from Harvard to Hollywood or from MIT to Menlo Park, but if you know you want to work in media or entertainment, being in LA or NYC is tough to beat. So NYU, Columbia, UCLA and USC are pretty great schools to consider…and why not—LA can be a very fun place to live (especially if you have a cool car).

It's really all about landing that first job. If you're not in the recruiting bulls eye for your target industry, you are just going to have to work harder to break into your chosen field. This is especially true if you're trying to do something outside the Consulting/ Banking/ Branding/ Technology mainstream. You can definitely make it happen, but it will require some shoe leather and a determination to GATGJ (Get After That Good Job).

Brand Name and Network

In choosing a business school, you are choosing which brand and school network to associate yourself with for years to come. While Harvard's alumni network is huge (*78,000* huge) and Stanford's is prestigious, you may not have all the access to them that you'd like. Or maybe they're in industries that don't interest you. Most of these top schools have lots of alumni on Wall Street or in consulting, but what if you want to go into entertainment or biotech? I'm not saying these aren't massively powerful networks (they are). I'm saying that it's important for you to understand what you're looking for and what each school has to offer. The more specialized your interests, the more your research will help you find your jam.

One thing to keep in mind regarding program brand is that as you consider schools further down the rankings, the perceived value of your degree is going to be correlated to the proximity to your alma mater. For example, people in the southeast think very highly of an Emory MBA and people in Indiana understand that a IU/Kelley MBA is a very good school, but that brand perception won't travel away from campus as well as Harvard, Stanford *et al.*

ZODIAC SIGN	BIRTHDATES	PERSONALITY TRAITS	SCHOOL FOR YOU:
Aries	Mar 21 - Apr 20	Assertive, intelligent, willful, impatient with others, frustrated by outside suggestions.	Booth, Sloan, HBS, Wharton
Taurus	Apr 21 - May 21	Self-confident, reliable, patient, determined, not a leader, sense of humor.	Law school
Gemini	May 22 - Jun 21	Social, curious, talkative, rational, mischievous.	Darden, Fuqua, Kellogg, Tuck, Anderson

ZODIAC SIGN	BIRTHDATES	PERSONALITY TRAITS	SCHOOL FOR YOU:
Cancer	Jun 22 - Jul 22	Tenacious, loyal, moody, independent.	Stern, Columbia
Leo	Jul 23 - Aug 21	Passionate, strong, arrogant, self-centered, success at any cost, wants to be treated like royalty.	HBS, Wharton
Virgo	Aug 22 - Sept 23	Analytical, well-read, loyal, self-effacing yet overly critical, creative.	Booth, Sloan, Tepper
Libra	Sept 24 - Oct 23	Charming, good-looking, diplomatic, gracious, has lots of friends.	Tuck
Scorpio	Oct 24 - Nov 22	Resourceful, bold, powerful, energetic, patient, brave.	Stanford, HBS
Sagittarius	Nov 23 - Dec 22	Risk-taker with a sense of humor, restless, impatient.	Wharton, Columbia, Stern, HBS (get into trading)
Capricorn	Dec 23 - Jan 20	Disciplined, prudent, serious, authoritative.	Booth, Sloan, Wharton
Aquarius	Jan 21 - Feb 19	Honest, loyal, idealistic, utopian, derives identity from groups, temperamental.	Haas
Pisces	Feb 20 - Mar 20	Perceptive, emotional, receptive, highly sensitive, dreamy, mystical, artistic.	Yale

Size Matters!

Top programs vary in size from the gigantic (HBS at 900+ per class) to those with around or under 200 (Emory, Vanderbilt, Indiana). Haas has just bumped its class size up 15% to 241, and the formerly petite Tuck is now 55% less cutesy-wutesy at 280 per class.

Class size affects all manner of things: where you live, how you relate to your classmates, how much attention you get from your professors and the kind of network you take away from school.

Smaller schools often emphasize the accessibility of their faculty, the tight-knit nature of the experience and the strong alumni network, but might be less well positioned to get the top recruiters or visiting executives to campus. I found Tuck's small class size to my liking, but there were those who felt stifled by its remoteness and intimacy.

Other downsides of modest-sized programs include the inability to ditch that one omnipresent loser in your class, a limited selection of potential romantic partners and everybody being all up in your bidness.

Many smaller programs don't lean as heavily on executive education revenue as do some of the bigger programs. They argue that this allows them to focus their resources on the full-time MBA candidate. This argument will resonate with you if you are half as narcissistic as I was (am).

On the other hand, more revenue allows for more faculty and increased course selection. At Wharton (with a juicy 859 students in its newest class), the list of Finance classes is longer than the menu at The Cheesecake Factory (which is really long, in case you're some kind of health freak who has never been to a delicious Cheesecake Factory). So there's a *lot* to choose from if you want to dive into the more exotic sub-topics of Finance.

More students also allows for more choices in international study opportunities and flexibility in program schedules, like the one year gig at Kellogg and Columbia's J-Term plan, wherein students start in January, skip a summer internship, then merge with the rest of the class for the second year curriculum.

So there are pros and cons related to class size. Familiarize yourself with them well enough to ask the right questions.

Here's how some of the top programs line up, size-wise:

- **500+:** Booth, Kellogg, Columbia, Wharton, HBS

- **300-499:** Yale, Darden, NYU, UCLA, MIT, Stanford, Duke, Michigan

- **<300:** Cornell, UNC, Tuck, Texas, Georgetown, Haas, Carnegie-Mellon, Indiana, Emory, Vanderbilt, USC, Wash U

Gender Balance

Perhaps the most positive recent trend at top programs is the increased presence of women in the classroom. Many of the leading schools (HBS, Wharton, Stanford, Tuck) have worked hard to raise the percentage of female class members to near or over 40%. This is a meaningful bump over only the past 2 years (Stanford up from 35% in 2013), but a huge increase over 10 or 20 years ago. Booth, for example, has more than doubled the 20% women in their Class of 2001 to 42% for the Class of 2016.[20]

The trend appears to have legs.

(Wait, that sounded wrong.)

What I mean is that it looks like the positive momentum will continue, as in the test year ending June 30, 2014, women made up 43.3% of GMAT test-takers, the highest percentage in GMAT history (source: GMAC 2015 *Data-to-Go*).

Interestingly, a great deal of this growth is coming from Asia, and China in particular. Of the top 25 countries in total GMAT tests, countries with the highest proportion of women taking the test are:

- China (65%),

- Taiwan (57%),

- Russia (53%),

- Thailand (58%) and

- Vietnam (59%).

---

20   http://www.forbes.com/sites/mattsymonds/2015/09/09/mba-students-of-2017-are-more-diverse-more-international-and-more-feminine-are-they-also-smarter/

The real driver of growth here is China, where the number of women taking the GMAT doubled from 2010 until 2014. Today China by itself represents 36% of *all* female prospective business school students around the world (GMAC).

And check this out—of the five total people who took the GMAT last year in Djibouti, Burundi and Curaçao combined, 100% were women. Bam! (GMAC).

Unfortunately, it's not across-the-board growth. The percentage of U.S. women taking the GMAT has remained at a relatively constant 40-41% over this time, but the total number is declining (GMAC). Much the same seems to be going on in Canada and Western Europe, where the percentages of women test-takers is slightly up, but the total number of female test-takers is relatively flat.

International Programs

What's the matter? U.S.A. not good enough for you? Fine, just go. Seriously, if you are looking for a career in international business, put INSEAD, LBS, IMD, IE, IESE or some other acronym on your list and get after it. That said, pretty much all top U.S. schools continue to invest in and expand their international consulting or study abroad opportunities. Do some research as to which one you like best. This is a good potential subject for your application essays, *ese*.

Big City v. Small Town

Figuring I would spend most of my career in colossal cities, I considered living in a small New England town for two years a really great / rare opportunity. Some alumni and students choose a remote location just to get out of the city for a couple of years. Either way, there's something wonderful about living in an idyllic setting like Hanover, Ithaca or Charlottesville (even if some of the sophisticated international students thought we all smelled like cow dung).

On the other hand, small schools that are hard to get to don't always attract as many recruiters who could see more students at larger programs by just taking the subway across town. (As if Goldman and McKinsey partners take the subway.)

I probably would have had better luck landing internships in media from NYU or Columbia, but I could not have learned to snow ski in Greenwich Village, as I did at the Dartmouth Skiway, just 20 minutes from the Tuck campus. By the way, if you think New England isn't a dangerous place to live then you have never braved New Hampshire's icy ski slopes.

Which schools are the most remote? To give you an idea, I fused data from Google Maps and *US News & World Report* and compiled the following table to give you a feel for it...

\multicolumn{6}{c}{US NEWS & WORLD REPORT'S TOP 10 MBA PROGRAMS RANKED BY PROXIMITY TO NEAREST CINNABON}					
RANK	SCHOOL	USNR RANKING	LOCATION	NEAREST CINNABON	MILES BY CAR
1	Wharton	3	Philadelphia, PA	Market Street Philadelphia, PA	2.4
2	Kellogg	6	Evanston, IL	Westfield Old Orchard, Skokie, IL	4.0
3	Columbia	8	New York, NY	Hackensack Plaza, Hackensack, NJ	10.3
4	Stanford	1	Stanford, CA	Sunnavale Town Center, Sunnyvale, CA	11.8
5	UC Berkeley	7	Berkeley, CA	Hilltop Mall, Richmond, CA	11.8
6	U Chicago	4	Chicago, IL	Chicago Ridge Mall, Chicago Ridge, IL	14.2
7	MIT	5	Cambridge, MA	Solomon Pond Mall, Marlborough, MA	33.4
8	Harvard	2	Boston, MA	Solomon Pond Mall, Marlborough, MA	37.4
9	Dartmouth	9	Hanover, NH	Mall of New Hampshire, Manchester, NH	86.0
10	UVA	10	Charlottesville, VA	Potomac Mills Shopping Center, Woodbridge, VA	93.0

(Please call store before venturing out. Cinnabons have a tendency to close without warning.)

Rankings: Do they matter?

OF COURSE they matter. But don't confuse rankings with universal truth.

On the one hand, rankings can help boost interest and confidence in up-and-coming programs. On the other hand, while Duke's Fuqua was #1 in *Business Week's* 2014 ratings and is a damn fine school, very few are going to pick Fuqua over Harvard or Stanford...*ceteris paribus*. By the way, in that same edition, *Business Week* ranked Harvard a lackluster #8. Yes, that's the Harvard Business School that you would murder your Aunt Mildred to attend.

Know this: rankings are produced to make the publisher money. Whether they are selling you a book, a magazine, or trying to drive traffic to their website, the publisher leverages rankings for earning more than learning. Sure, the significant revenues driven by applicants' / students' / alumni's obsession with (and thus schools' angst over) these reasoned but still somewhat arbitrary numbers creates editorial budgets for more in-depth coverage than the subject would garner otherwise...*ceteris paribus*.

So who does the ranking? *US News and World Report, Bloomberg-Businessweek, The Economist,* the *Financial Times.* In other words, the biggest names in business news—and these reports are all very competitive with each other.

Publishing the same list of schools in the same order every year (or in the same order as your competitors) wouldn't be news. So, there has to be change, which means some schools win and some schools lose in each year's new rankings.

Yale SOM went from #21 in *Businessweek's* 2012 rankings to #6 in 2014. Yes, they got an incredible new building, but did the long-term value of a Yale diploma really change that much in just two years? Likely no more than the quality of pizza in New Haven (which is outstanding, btw).

Fuqua's surge to #1 in 2014 was a five spot jump up from their previous ranking of #6. They then dropped back to #8 in 2015. The rankings are like dating a crazy person who screams, "I hate you! I love you! I hate you!" You have to count to 10, create a healthy distance, and say, "This just isn't working out."

Furthermore, the process of ranking is fraught with methodological risks. Rely too much on objective data (admit rates, GMAT scores, average total compensation three years after graduation), and the process becomes a self-fulfilling prophecy (the highest ranking schools get lots of the best applicants who go on to make the most money, and so on). Use too much subjective data (surveys filled out by students and alumni), and it turns into a gigantic horn-blowing contest.

Do rankings matter? Yes. But take them as directional and as only one of many data points.

PROGRAMS BY REPUTATION[21]

KUMBAYA / HIPPY LOVE FESTS—MOST COLLABORATIVE SCHOOLS:

- Yale
- Tuck
- UNC
- Kellogg

"DON'T MESS WITH ME."—MOST COMPETITIVE SCHOOLS:

- Wharton
- Columbia
- Vanderbilt (*whaaa?*)
- Harvard

---

21   Source: aggregation of multiple sources.

"YO, VINNY!"—BIG-CITY SCHOOLS (MOST LIKELY RUN BY THE MOB)

- Columbia
- NYU
- Harvard
- Wharton

"YOU GOT A PURTY MOUTH"—SMALL TOWN LOCATIONS

- Tuck
- Cornell
- Darden

CHAPTER 9

SCHOOL REVIEWS

I AM HERE TO BE OF SOME VALUE TO YOU, KIND READER (NOT a ton of value. But some). In this section I will share what I believe, have been led to believe, have read or have been told to be (part of) the truth behind the top business school programs.

I come to these beliefs from 100+ hours of research on school websites, student blogs, MBA message boards, 125 alumni/student surveys and the usual suspects of major business periodicals' rankings, as discussed in the previous chapter.

I have no agenda other than sharing what is widely considered to be true (and, in some cases, funny), even if it's the kind of thing that schools will not mention in their marketing materials.

Please know that there is just too much going on at all of these programs to try to summarize in a couple hundred words, bullets and jokey jokes. As brilliant as my thoughts and observations are, they should be taken with a giant grain of salt.

You too should synthesize as much data as possible into a comprehensive, if imperfect, picture. Then go visit the campuses that seem like the best fit for you. Talk to as many students, alumni, faculty and recruiters as possible. One program may be perceived to be "better" than another, but that doesn't mean that it's a better fit for you and your career.

Following are broad descriptions of the top U.S. programs.

TRANSPARENCY IN ACTION: CALLING OUT MY OWN PERSONAL BIAS

- **UVA**: Their short-sighted admissions offices wait-listed me *twice* (once for undergrad and once for Darden). Can you believe that? I know, me neither (or either—whatever). Apparently they're not impressed with profanity in application essays. Uppity jerks. For the record, they also denied Dr. Seuss.

- **Wharton / Harvard:** I have a huge inferiority complex, so I bash you harder. Impress me with your sense of humor.

- **Stanford:** I worked in the Bay Area a long time with a lot of these Stanford smarty-pantses…most of whom were actually very cool. But not all. #TimKendall.

- **Tuck:** I went to Tuck and loved it. If you think my bias is unfair to your school then spend a year of your life writing your own satirical b-school guidebook.

- **Princeton:** Doesn't even have a business school, but they rejected me pretty hard for undergrad, so screw them.

Note: Getting bounced by UVA and Princeton in the undergrad admission process pissed me off and hurt my feelings (sad face emoticon), but it also steeled my resolve such that I was determined to get into a great business school. I used that negative experience as inspiration to push myself toward my best work. So when you grow tired of studying for the GMAT or you find yourself thinking that your application essays are "good enough" before they are, find something in your past—good or bad—that fires you up enough to push through until you are doing your very best work.

SCHOOL REVIEWS

The data cited in this section are for the most recently admitted class since 2015 and comes from school websites/Twitter feeds, *US News*, *Poets & Quants*, MBAmission.com, *The Economist*, Wikipedia, GMATclub.com message boards, Quora, BusinessInsider, mba50. com and the American Kennel Club. Quotes/ observations/ conjecture comes from surveys of business school alumni and students.

THE TOP DOZEN
(in alphabetical order...sort of)

University of Chicago Booth
School of Business

★ (AKA, "Booth," "Chicago-Booth," or "Frankie")

★ 42% Women

★ 34% International

★ 23% Minority

★ Average GMAT—726

★ Lots of engineering and science undergrad majors, mixed in with the usual Business/Econ majors

★ Weather: Painfully cold

★ Student nickname: Boothies

Ranked #1 in the most recent report by *The Economist* and historically near the top of all the rankings, Booth is a high-powered quantitative boot camp, well known for its academic rigor and customizable curriculum.

Booth is very much the global enterprise with not only 585 students in the latest full-time MBA class, but with evening, executive, PhD and part-time MBAs spread over campuses in Chicago, Miami, London, Hong Kong and Singapore.

Unlike most other top programs, there are no cohorts at Booth, which may be one of the reasons Booth has a reputation for being less chummy than other top schools. School leaders offer that "Booth is a place of community, not conformity," perhaps to distinguish it from cross-town rival Kellogg or other relatively "squishy" programs like Stanford and Tuck. One Booth student reported to *Businessweek* that he made 1,500 lifelong friends at Booth, which is either complete bullcrap from someone who's supposed to be good at math or utter delusion from the kind of person who friends you on Facebook as soon as he meets you.[22]

With so many crazy smart students trained in the world's second oldest business school, it's not surprising that top firms are falling all over themselves to hire Boothies.

Thirty percent of Booth's Class of '14 went into consulting, with McKinsey, Bain and BCG hiring over 16% of the entire class (CAUTION: consulting nerd boner ahead). Another 41% went into some kind of finance, with over a third of those going into investment banking.

You might not think of Booth as a marketing school, but 9.5% went into the field immediately after graduation, a similar portion as that of other schools better known for consumer products. 'Attaboy, Frankie!

- Quirk: As one alum put it, "Nobel prize winners who teach. Incredibly intellectual environment. Crazy academics—I mean really crazy."
- Secret Sauce: Boothies get to wear t-shirts with Milton Friedman silhouettes on them.
- Strengths: Chicago is a blast. Food, music, arts, bars. Friendly people. Great golf (three months out of the year).
- Threats: Hypothermia.
- Famous alumni: Satya Nadella (CEO of Microsoft), Jon Corzine (former Goldman-Sachs CEO and former Governor of New Jersey), Pete Peterson (Founder of Blackstone Group), David Booth (recognize the name?), and lots, lots more stoopid rich brainiacs.

Columbia Business School

★ 36% women
★ 35% minority

---

22 http://www.bloomberg.com/bw/articles/2014-11-11/best-business-schools-2014-by-the-numbers

* ★ 42% International
* ★ GMAT average: 715
* ★ Half the class came from Financial Services or Consulting backgrounds (a measurement also known as "The Misery Index")
* ★ Weather: Bleh
* ★ Student Nickname: CBSers (very clever)
* ★ 25% from Financial Services
* ★ 23% from Consulting
* ★ 8% from Private Equity

Columbia University may have been the fertile crescent of the Beat Generation, but it's now the home of a super-competitive, hot-shit business school. One recent graduate going into the consulting industry received a $1 million signing bonus. Let me repeat: One. Million. Effing. Dollars.[23]

Columbia's upper Upper West Side location earns its legit NYC cred, with all the rights, benefits and detriments thereto pertaining. Which means CBS boasts some 500 guest lecturers every year, and that right outside the business school facilities—at this very moment—there is a dude taking a dump on the sidewalk.

* ✎ Secret Sauce: Location means you are one subway ride from Wall Street, Madison Avenue and the best delis on G-d's green earth. Strong international contingent.
* ✎ Quirk: Columbia Follies are amazing. If you have not yet seen "The Munger Games" video on YouTube, you should Google it right now.
* ✎ Strengths: New York City. Tons of visiting stars from the business world. Access to the world's biggest movers/shakers. Great international study opportunities. Also, there is a new Century 21 (discount designer clothes) at

---

23   http://www.bloomberg.com/bw/articles/2014-11-11/best-business-schools-2014-by-the-numbers

Broadway and 66th that's just a few stops down on the 1 Train.

✎ Weaknesses: CBS' current facilities blow. Sparkly fresh facilities are coming as part of the CU expansion onto a new 17-acre Manhattanville campus. Henry Kravis (alum whose name is synonymous with private equity) and Ron Perelman (not an alum, but uber-wealthy PE guy also), both gave $100 million to kick off the campaign.

✎ Opportunities: To renovate its messy website, which offers its digital visitor the opportunity to "download a brochure." (How 'bout you just fax it to me?) Worse—the information on the brochure is data from the entering class of 2012— (i.e., four years out-of-date). This excellent program deserves much better marketing.

University of Virginia Darden School of Business

★ 32% women
★ 16% Domestic Minorities
★ Average GMAT: 706
★ Weather: Better than average. Amazing in spring and fall
★ Student nickname: Dardenites

University of Virginia's excellent school of business, Darden, has a new, fired-up dean who is comin' straight outta McKinsey. He inherits a great teaching faculty at a school steeped in tradition. A recent emphasis on experiential learning augments the case method, the historical academic foundation of the Darden experience.

Darden is known for its hardcore, case-centric curriculum, intense workload and cohesive student body on an elegant campus in magnificent Charlottesville, VA.

Darden augments its small town location with school-sponsored job treks, international student exchange programs, global consulting projects and significant global coursework (focused on Argentina, Brazil, China, India, Spain, among other countries).

Half of Darden graduates go directly into consulting or financial services, but a bakers' dozen in the Class of '14 went to work at Amazon.

- ✐ Quirk: The whole "Mr. Jefferson's University" thing (fawning tribute to UVA founder, Thomas "TJ" Jefferson) can be a bit heavy-handed, but give the guy credit—he believed in wine, architecture and romance. Oh yeah, and in the revolutionary concept of representative democracy. Speaking of politics, famous Darden alumni include Mark Sanford, former SC governor whose spokesperson in 2009 told the world he was hiking the Appalachian Trail, when he was actually in Buenos Aires with his mistress. TJ would be proud.
- ✐ Secret Sauce: Tight student body and alumni network born out of a rigorous, bonding experience in an intimate setting.
- ✐ Can't Miss Class: Mr. Jefferson's Guide to Crisis Management 304: Minimizing the Fallout from Executive Paternity Suits.
- ✐ Strengths: Charlottesville is small, but it's also home to almost 15,000 undergrads, so it's got the all the arts, dining and athletics (i.e. beer pong) that comes along with a groovy college town. Good Housekeeping named C-ville the happiest city in America.
- ✐ Opportunities: Increase student diversity.

Duke—Fuqua School of Business:

* Women: 35%
* International: 40%
* Minority: 21%
* GMAT Range (middle 80%): 640-750
* Student nickname: Fuquans

Born in 1969, Fuqua is one of the youngest top MBA programs, but has achieved great status in its short 46-year life.

The school has a ton of momentum in the rankings, landing *Numero Uno* in *BusinessWeek*'s 2014 poll, thanks to employers' enthusiasm for Fuqua alums' ability to work in teams. Add in good weather, a cool small city and being a part of Duke University, and you've got a bunch of great reasons to consider Fuqua.

Like Kellogg, Fuqua is all about collaboration. There is no "I" in "Team Fuqua," which means—among other things—*Supportive Ambition* and *Loyal Community*. School leadership states it clearly: "*We are a family who looks out for each other. Team Fuqua has got your back when you need it the most.*"

Read that again.

In a world obsessed by short-term bottom lines and success at any cost, that is a refreshing thing to stand for—especially in the training of future business leaders. Such optimism and support comes through in student satisfaction. Surveys of Fuquans are so overwhelmingly positive you might think that someone is pumping the Fuqua HVAC with nitrous-oxide.

The Fuqua admission team works hard to recruit students who are both smart and interesting. Their application includes the essay question commanding applicants to list 25 random things about themselves (see the related list on page 179).

Their work seems to have paid off. Recent members of the incoming class include:

✍ The inventor of The Keg Koozy (now that's innovation!)

- ✐ A math lover who has memorized Pi to more than 500 places (a party trick that even a Boothie or a Sloanie could respect)
- ✐ A third generation Special Forces Green Beret (I'm not going to make a joke about this dude because his grandpa might come after me)
- ✐ A competitive eater (who, after a year at Fuqua will be known as a "collaborative eater"), and...
- ✐ A stand-up comedian (whose career is obviously screwed)

Future unemployed comedians not withstanding, Fuqua places grads in all the right places. Big chunks of the class of '14 went directly into the following functions: 34% Consulting (31 to Deloitte, 14 to BCG and PWC, 12 to McKinsey, 10 to Accenture), 24% Finance and 21% Marketing. Interesting top employers outside of the professional services world include Microsoft (16), Amazon (10), Samsung (10), Google (6).

- ✐ Quirk: Student nickname is definitely not "Fuquads." DEFINITELY NOT.
- ✐ Secret Sauce: Coach K. The legendary Duke basketball coach has his own institute here: The Fuqua/Coach K Center of Leadership & Ethics (COLE). Pretty cool, 'eh.
- ✐ Can't Miss Class: Human Resources 201: Dealing with Rich, Entitled Punks (an immersive, interactive experience with Duke undergrads).
- ✐ Strengths: General management, team-oriented, cool classmates.
- ✐ Opportunities: Make Duke football better.
- ✐ Notable Alumni: Tim Cook, CEO of Apple, Melinda Gates.

Haas School of Business, University of California Berkeley

★ 41% Women

★ 40% International

★ 36% U.S. Minority

★ Average GMAT: 715

★ Middle 80%: 680-760

★ Industries represented in the incoming class include:

   o 24% Consulting

   o 19% Banking / Finserv

   o 5% Technology, which seems low considering its location and that Stanford's class has 3x that percentage

If writing this book opened my eyes to the competitiveness of any program, it has been Berkeley-Haas. Perhaps because of its neighbor Stanford's long shadow or because Haas was fighting its way into the top 10 rankings in the early 1990s when I was applying to schools, Haas just wasn't on my radar.

But the school is here to stay—and party—with a 715 average GMAT and 13.2% admit rate that make Haas one of the most selective programs in the U.S.

And what's not to love? Berkeley is totally gorj and located within easy striking distance of the most exciting companies in the world. Oh sure, Berkeley is crunchy and was home to the Symbionese Liberation Army, but what was that but a well-armed start-up disrupting the banking industry?

Some of that historical counter-culture flavor peaks its way into the experience. Haas' Number 1 Defining Principle is "Question the Status Quo" (whoa, dude!). Number 4 is "Beyond Yourself," which encourages graduates to lead "ethically and responsibly." Almost 4% of recent graduates went directly into non-profit work.

And check out this stat: a whopping 43.4% from Class of '14 took jobs in the Technology industry right after graduation. That's gigantic!

With another 26.4% going into consulting, that's damn near 70% of the class going into only two industries. It's impressive almost to the point of being a liability (what happens if there's a downturn in tech?). Btw, one hears Haas' real estate program touted, but less than .5% of the class goes into the field.

At 240 people per class, Haas' full-time program is on the smaller side, but it's part of a much larger school that hosts part time and executive MBA candidates. Haas is adding 30% more facility space to handle more students and the program's significant momentum.

- Quirks: Dirty Berkeley hippies (like bestselling business author Michael Lewis). About Berkeley's political environment, one alumna writes that on any given day, "you never knew if there was going to be a riot, stand-in, or protest..."
- Secret Sauce: Speaking of sauce, you have to try Alice Waters' yummy Chez Panisse, a Berkeley treasure.
- Weaknesses: Social life described as "engineers gone wild."
- Opportunities: Continue to gain ground on Stanford.

Harvard Business School

- ★ Acceptance rate: 11%
- ★ 41% Women
- ★ 34% International
- ★ 28% U.S. Ethnic Minorities
- ★ GMAT middle 80%: 700-760
- ★ Median GMAT: 730 (ka-pow!)

* Weather: Bleh
* Student nickname: Cobra Kai
* Pre-School industries:
    * 18% from Venture Capital and Private Equity (no kidding!)
    * 82% Other

Considering HBS? You think you're pretty special, don't you? DON'T YOU!! Well good for you. Yes, Harvard is the place for people who think they're special and appreciate the cultural amenities of Massachusetts.

For the rest of your life when people ask you where you went to business school, you can answer "Harvard. Ever heard of it?" And it will feel sooooo good.

HBS is a big, Mac Daddy business school brand and a literally *big* business school. Nine hundred students per class and 90 per cohort means it's not exactly intimate. And while it's not cutthroat either, one still has to fight to stand out in the crowd. But anyone who has the stuff to gain admission to this roiling stew of world class business ninjas can find a way to distinguish herself.

It's not as if HBS students lack confidence. One HBS alumnus answered my survey question "Why did you apply to your alma mater?" with "Best one out there." Which would have been fine (hey, he *should* be proud to have gone to HBS), except that he then included a smiley face emoticon. Now come on—you are either a bad-ass or you are not. And bad-asses do not use emoticons—they only make parenthetical reference to where emoticons should be (like right here).

    🖉 Secret Sauce: Dropping "The H-Bomb" (i.e., telling potential romantic interests that you go to HBS). While it's incredibly douchy, I wish I coulda done it, but there was no equivalent to this at Dartmouth (which is probably fine because "Dropping the D-Bomb" sounds creepy).

🖉 Can't Miss Class: Managing Expectations 101: Your Ego Relative to Your Actual Value to the World.

🖉 Strengths: No matter what the polls say, Harvard is way up at the tippy-top in graduate management education brands.[24] Think of it this way—HBS is "The Harvard of business schools" (like, literally).

🖉 Weaknesses: I asked several HBS alums what they thought were the program weaknesses. They came back with answers like "Can't think of any," and "What do you mean, 'weaknesses'?" So there's your answer.

🖉 Threats: Exec Ed classes encroaching (like at most big schools with a robust exec ed presence). In a recent HBS Show (like Follies at other schools), the video joked that one of the main halls at HBS was closed to MBAs because there was an "Exec Ed Zumba class in session." Then again, all HBS alums get lifetime discounts to HBS Executive Education classes. Par-tay!!!!

🖉 HBS seeks applicants who demonstrate "The Habit of Leadership." And their alumni body certainly contains gigantic world leaders. Notable Alumni include George W. Bush, Meg Whitman, Jeffrey Immelt, Michael Bloomberg and a vast, global collection of übermenschen and über-womenschen. (If you're keeping score, that's one Nietzsche reference v. a whole chapter on Beavis & Butthead.)

Kellogg School of Management at Northwestern University

★ 43% women
★ 40% international
★ 23% US Minority

---

24   I wrote this just to piss off the Stanford and Wharton alums.

* Average GMAT: 724 (so study, yo)
* Weather: Chicago winter is nasty, brutish and long
* Student nickname: Kelloggians

One of the best brands in all of management education, Kellogg is known for producing smart, hard-working and friendly graduates.

The program is cohort-centric, stressing teamwork and collaboration. Like, a lot. The downside of mandated team work (you will work as a team and you will like it!), as one alum puts it, is that "it often feels more like jury work—because there's always the lone standout lunatic arguing for the smiley face logo."

Nonetheless, the teamwork and focus on cohorts seems to be paying off, as Kellogg students and alums—who are known to be a fun group—LOVE the freaking place. Maybe it's because Kellogg takes extra special care in the admissions process, requiring interviews before admitting an applicant. They do so to fulfill the clearly unreasonable expectation that all Kellogians have a personality.

Time management is a key priority at any top program, but it seems especially so at Kellogg, which is a frothy cornucopia of academic and extracurricular opportunities.

There are too many to list in one place, but among the hundreds of ways to expand your world at Kellogg, consider: Global Learning and Management programs, E-commerce immersion projects, Entrepreneurship Through Acquisition conference (co-hosted with Booth), the Super Bowl Ad Review (in which 70 students participate in the real time, multi-variable grading of commercials during the big game), the SpecialK Revue sketch comedy show or the annual Kellogg ski trip, which is attended by 750 students and significant others. To say nothing of dozens of other clubs, outings, charity events or just drinking beer in the bleachers at Wrigley Field.

Containing this madness requires great facilities and Kellogg is working on upgrading theirs. A new, 400,000 square foot home for the full-time MBA program opens in early 2017.

Kellogg's career services get extremely high marks from alumni and recruiters. The school is synonymous with marketing excellence, and if you want to "do marketing," you can't do any better. But as one alumnus says, Kellogg is more accurately described as "a strategy school that is known for marketing."

That assertion proves out in the employment numbers from the Class of '14, which sent 35% into consulting, 14% into financial services and 18.4% into technology (to primo destinations like Apple, Amazon and Microsoft).

- Secret Sauce: History as the top marketing school on the planet. Expanding its legacy into technology, consulting and entrepreneurship.
- Quirks: No classes on Wednesdays means Tuesday is the big night out. Academically, alumni report that it's "easy to get a B, but hard to get an A."
- Strengths: In beautiful Evanston, a leafy Chicago suburb. Kellogg is "a ton of fun."
- Weaknesses: Very purple, which is regal...but come on.

MIT Sloan School of Management

- ★ 41% women
- ★ 38% International
- ★ 33% Engineering undergrad majors (uh oh)
- ★ 14% Science and Math undergrad majors
- ★ Weather: Crappy to not-so-crappy
- ★ Town: Amazing
- ★ Graduate Reputation: Wicked smaht, numbers-oriented operators

Okay, first, there's MIT's classic academic location in Cambridge, MA, right on the Charles River, with its postcard view of the McLaurin Building's Great Dome. Second…well, there really isn't a second. You're part of MIT—what the hell else do you want?

When you matriculate to Sloan, you become part of America's preeminent polytechnic university. Their motto in Latin is *Mens et Manus*, which roughly translated means either "mind and hand" or "there ain't no better school nowhere" (my Latin is a bit rusty).

Either way, at Sloan, you are among the brightest, most creative whiz kids on the planet. The student rap on Sloan is that the d-bag factor is low, but the nerd factor is high (even for business school). But that's totally okay, because nerds run the world now—and that domination appears to have a lot of runway.

As one student reported, "…once I saw the MIT campus, I knew this was the place for me. The geekiness and culture was impossible to match."

Sloan articulates their approach not-so-subtly on their website: "We seek thought-leaders with exceptional intellectual abilities and the drive and determination to put their stamp on the world." Which really means "We recruit savants who are going to take over the freaking world!!!"

How do they do it? Through hardcore quantitative analytics and Action Learning, and MIT's unique "ongoing, iterative sequence of theory, practice and reflection" that combines classroom learning and real world application.

But it's not all Dungeons, Dragons and Bunsen burners at Sloan. Social life and extracurriculars abound. In addition to Thursday night C-Functions, the weekly school-wide cocktail parties that follow themes of the organizing student groups (e.g. Latin Club, Korean Club, LGBT Club), Sloan also has some of the quirkiest clubs and bad-ass conferences of any top school, for example:

- ✎ The (unofficial) Sloan Survival Club: A self-defense taught by ex-Navy Seal classmates and Sloanies who are MMA-fighters.

- The MIT $100k Entrepreneurship Competition: One of the world's largest and most prestigious business plan contests. Alumni of this competition have raised hundreds of millions of dollars in funding for their companies.
- The MIT Sloan Sports Analytics Conference: If you are a sports buff or liked the book/movie *Moneyball* then SAC will make you crap your pants with excitement. The event attracts players, coaches and senior front office staff from 80+ pro sports teams along with press, students and other obsessed sports statisticians. Bill James, creator of Sabermetrics and the father of baseball statistical analysis, called the conference the "culmination of 30 years of my work."

Another one of the cool things about Sloan is the Independent Activities Period (all of January). During IAP, students can do global study, conduct industry immersions or take classes on robotics, bio-engineering, film, Military leadership or—get this— Poker Theory and Analytics, which culminates in a tournament with thousands of dollars in non-cash prizes.

Not surprisingly, Sloan grads are leaders in their fields. Class of '14 saw 29.2% head into consulting, 17% go to High Tech and 10.2% go into retail (because when I think "MIT," I think "fashion").

- Notable alumni include: UN Secretary General Kofi Anan, Benjamin Netanyahu (who is the freaking Prime Minister of Israel...in case you didn't know), Former Hewlett-Packard CEO and Presidential candidate, Carly Fiorina, and a dazzling panoply of CEOs, founders and other monsters of intellect.
- Strengths: Hardcore analytical program that attracts brilliant students and trains them into phenomenal operators.

Stanford Graduate School o' Business

★ Acceptance Rate: 6.5% (yikes!)
★ 40% Women
★ 40% International
★ 19% U.S. Minority
★ GMAT range: 570[25]-800
★ GMAT mean: 733 (yikes again)
★ Weather: Amazing
★ 15% from Technology
★ 8% from Financial Services
★ 16% from Consulting
★ 16% from Venture capital or private equity
★ 6% from Entertainment/Media
★ 13% from Government/Non-profit
★ 17% of grads go into start-ups

Okay, we're going to try something a little different to describe Stanford GSB, the most competitive school in the set. Ripping off David Letterman, here are the Top 6 Reasons to Go to GSB:

6. Silicon Valley: If you think you're special *and* you have an idea for a world-changing digital company, you gotta go to Stanford! You'll study within sneezing range of Apple, Mark Zuckerberg and the Google fellas. You will be stalked by angel investors and venture capital grows like kudzu on Sand Hill Road, adjacent to the Stanford campus.

5. Facilities: The new-ish, awesome Knight Management Center, which is named for GSB alum and Nike founder, Phil Knight.

4. Weather: From the GSB website: "Northern California enjoys a Mediterranean climate. Temperatures average

---

25   Clearly a legacy.

60 to 70 degrees Fahrenheit all year round. Morning fog usually gives way to sunshine during the days, and evenings are crisp and cool." True as this may be, I read this while sweating in a steaming Atlanta August and can't help thinking, "Oh fuck you, Northern California! I hope you're enjoying your drought."

3. **A stunning alumni network** that includes (in addition to Mr. Knight) Charles Schwab, Nolan Bushnell (who founded both Atari AND Chuck E. Cheese), HBO CEO Jeff Bewkes, GM CEO Mary Barras, the CEOs or former CEOs of Wells-Fargo, Anheuser Busch-InBev, BP, Capital One, General Mills, Abbot Labs and many more members of the corporate glitterati.

2. **Location:** Stanford is less than two hours from Napa/ Sonoma, Carmel and the Oakland Raiders. It's also a short 40 minutes up to magnificent San Francisco (150 minutes with traffic).

1. **Weed:** Is basically legal in Palo Alto.

✎ Secret Sauce: Their logo is a tree. So there's that.

✎ Can't Miss Class: Silicon Valley 206: How to be All Disrupt-y And Stuff.

✎ Strengths: Too many to list. If you get into GSB but choose not to attend, you're an idiot.

✎ Weaknesses: Coming to the realization that, after getting into and graduating from Stanford, the only skill that really matters in Silicon Valley is the ability to write code. What's that you say—that business development is a valuable skill? Please tell me you're kidding.

✎ Threats: Cost-of-living in Bay Area. Average first year compensation for a graduate in last year's class was $170,000. While this is a staggering sum, keep in mind that that's only like $56,000 after California state taxes and that average annual rent in The Bay Area will consume most of your net.

✎ Quirk: There's a sushi restaurant in downtown Palo Alto that serves a "Stanford Roll," which is rice wrapped around cream cheese, salmon roe and thinly-sliced cardinal. It's delicious.

Tuck School of Business, Dartmouth College

* ★ 42% women (up from 32%)
* ★ 32% International
* ★ 20% U.S. Minorities
* ★ 24% from Consulting
* ★ 15% from Financial Services
* ★ 12% from Investment banking and PE
* ★ Weather: Damn cold
* ★ Student nickname: Tuckies

Do you want to work your ass off in the freezing woods? Is proximity to moose and black bears an important factor in choosing a business school? Do you have earthy hazel eyes that match the school's Dartmouth green paraphernalia? Then Tuck is the place for you.

The birthplace of the MBA (just sayin'), Tuck is known for its cohesive student body, great faculty and focus on the full-time MBA candidates. There are no undergrads and relatively few executive MBAs mucking about. Case-centric curriculum is intense in first year, but lightens considerably in the second year.

A 33% increase in the percentage of women in Tuck's most recent class will mean a better balance of power in the dating dynamics. "Buy and hold" has traditionally been the only effective dating strategy if one wants to stay warm during the long winter nights. And while romantic leverage still skews female, the previous disproportionate demand gave women what renowned business strategist Michael Porter might describe as meaningful "supplier power." Perhaps the threat of substitutes will level the playing field.

Tuckies socialize together (what choice have they got?) and are very much into outdoor activities, such as hiking, ice hockey and skiing. The tight-knit community helps each other out. "Before accounting exams, the CPAs go around asking if anyone needs help." Some alums report the student body to be "homogenous," and some recruiters complain that Tuckies are "too nice." You've read this far in this book—do I seem that nice?

- Quirk: "Drinking. Lots of drinking." Habitrail-like tunnels that connect dorms to classrooms, dining halls and offices, thus allowing students to stay indoors all winter.
- Secret Sauce: Two years in delightful Hanover will refresh your soul...right before you sell it to pay off your student loans.
- Can't Miss Class: Acclimatizing 202: Strategies for Re-Adjusting to the Filthy Outside World After Graduation.
- Strengths: Hanover is beautiful. Professors are brilliant and accessible. The student body is very supportive, and the alumni network is the real deal. Best of all: you don't need a refrigerator to keep your beer cold. You just leave it outside in the snow.
- Weaknesses: Winter gets old after five or six months. Somewhat remote campus doesn't get all the action that a Columbia or a Harvard gets.
- Opportunities: To expand its global footprint while staying true to its identity, which is pretty awesome. As Conan O'Brien says about Dartmouth, it's Harvard and Yale's "sexually confident lacrosse-playing younger sibling who knows how to throw a party, and looks good in a down vest."

UCLA Anderson School of Management

★ Women: 30%

★ International: 33%

★ Minorities: 27%

★ Average GMAT: 714

★ GMAT middle 80%: 680-750

You clearly want to be an actor. And, dude/ma'am, if there were any justice in the world, you would be on TV right now. But unlike most actors, you know how to use Excel! So lower your expectations and celebrate the fact that you can be an agent! Or lower them further and go into biz dev for a major studio or large web property! Attending Anderson is great preparation for this. And look on the bright side: as MBA candidates go, you're gorgeous!

Okay, okay, this is all a stereotype. While Anderson is indeed strong in entertainment, 28% of Anderson's Class of '14 went into technology (more than Stanford's 24%) v. the relatively small 7.4% who go into media / entertainment.

In fact, Anderson sends grads of its strong program into lots of different fields (perhaps the most evenly-divided of the top schools). With 16.3% headed to consulting and just under 10% to investment banking, the balance head toward jobs in a mix of consumer products, real estate, healthcare, education, energy and more.

This healthy distribution of alumni industries is due, at least in part, to Anderson students' ability to customize their schedules and choose from specialization tracks in one of the following: Accounting, Brand Management, Corporate Finance, Tech Leadership, Entertainment, Entrepreneurship, Global Management, Healthcare, Investment Management, Sustainability, Marketing Analytics or Real Estate.

✎ Secret Sauce: Access to internships in nearby Beverly Hills and Hollywood. Super-hot undergrads.

✐ Can't Miss Class: Talent Agency 101: How to Drive a Mercedes S550 While Making $41,000 per year.

✐ Strengths: Sick (good) weather, dude. "Students tend to be happy here and social life in LA is great."

✐ Strengths Also: Celebrity sightings. The Coffee Bean. Zankou Chicken. The top program closest to Lionel Richie's house. The spirit of John Wooden. Mark Cuban's Landmark Theatre, just down Westwood Blvd. Everyone looks good in blue and gold!

✐ Famous Anderson alumni include Bill Gross (Founder of PIMCO), Susan Wojcicki (CEO of YouTube) and the CEOs of Target, Deloitte Consulting and AEG.

The Wharton School of the University of Pennsylvania

★ 42% women

★ 35% International

★ 30% U.S. Students of Color

★ GMAT range 630-790

★ GMAT mean 725

★ Weather: Bleh

★ Class came from following industries:
    ★ 12% from Investment Banking
    ★ 12% from Private Equity /Venture Capital
    ★ 8% from "other financial services" (bank tellers?)
    ★ 68% NOT Finance

★ Student nicknames: Whartonites

If you want to end up on Wall Street, *you must consider Wharton*. It is a fecund breeding ground for incipient bankers and other motivated, smart-as-hell ass-kickers, so strap in and hold on.

As a Wharton Deputy Dean told *Poets & Quants* in an interview a few years ago, "We do not have a charisma-style approach. We let the data drive us…" In other words, if you understand numbers better than people, Wharton is the place for you (smiley emoticon).

In fairness, Wharton's "finance only" rep is overblown. Check this out—*US News* recently ranked Wharton #2 in Marketing, right behind Kellogg. And though 35% of last year's class did go directly into financial services, Wharton lands graduates in top gigs across a variety of industries and functions. Twenty-six percent from the Class of '14 went into consulting, 7.5% into consumer products, 13.7% into technology and almost 6% into healthcare. Notable that 2.2% went into real estate, which is a lot like finance (because one should know how to use a calculator).

Plus, at Wharton, you are legit Ivy League and part of the University of Pennsylvania, with its deep tradition and history, though they don't overdo it. If Wharton students had as big a stiffy for their founder (Benjamin Franklin) as UVA students have for Thomas Jefferson, they'd all be walking around flying kites with fake bald pates on their heads.

Notable Wharton alumni include a *ridiculous* number of business super-heroes who, when pictured together, make The Justice League look like a bunch of slobbering morons.

Yet know that if you attend Wharton, you'll be going to school with people who name their pets "Black Scholes" and "Jamie Dimon" (even though he went to HBS). Prepare to hear, "Hello, I'm Sven, and this is my Maltese, Berkshire Hathaway Buffett."

- ✐ Secret Sauce: Hard-core finance training and decades of leadership on Wall Street. A giant selection of courses in finance and marketing.
- ✐ Can't Miss Class: Post-grad Home Economics 306: Engaging the Right REALTORs®, Home Chefs and Wardrobe Consultants in Greenwich, CT.
- ✐ Strengths: Philadelphia (close to New York, but not actually in New York, great restaurants and grimy late

night cheesesteaks). The very high likelihood that you will be an enormously wealthy person within a few years. ROI: "($140k) for a guaranteed higher Earning Potential spouse—it's a no brainer!" (Written by a gold-digging male Wharton grad.)

✎ Weaknesses: Philadelphia. This is the town that booed Santa Claus. "And the love/hate relationship Center City residents have with 1,600 boisterous MBAs."

✎ Quirk: "Raging, over-the-top partying" dominated "by fabulous foreigners from Latin America and Europe."

ROUNDING OUT THE TOP 25

Keep in mind what I said before: arbitrary lines are drawn when making lists. There is no absolute truth to my inclusion, exclusion or batching of any particular program in the "Top 25." Some that aren't listed here arguably should have made the list. Some that follow should arguably be in the top dozen. Then again, some schools not listed here aren't that great.

Here's the next baker's dozen…

NYU Stern School of Business

Smack-dab in the middle of NYC's Greenwich Village, Stern's got probably the coolest location of any business school in the world. It is literally around the corner from head shops, shwarma stands, The Comedy Cellar (the epicenter of U.S. comedy), the world's top digital companies, advertising agencies, Wall Street and some guy masturbating on his stoop at 10:00 a.m. Stern's 720 Average GMAT and 16% admit rate means admission is highly competitive. Stern features great finance, entertainment, media and digital programs, but 28% go into consulting and 27% go into investment banking.

- ★ Can't Miss Class: Greenwich Village Commodities Trading 201: Buying Drugs in Washington Square Park While Selling Plasma to Pay Stern Tuition
- ★ Weaknesses: Too close to New Jersey
- ★ Quotes: "The best school in New York with the lowest 'jerk' factor" (I think she meant "d-bag," but you get the point)

University of Michigan's Ross School of Business

You're smart, love beer and want a big school experience with unbeatable college sports programs. Be sure to buy some nice sweaters and long johns because good, holy Lord is it cold. Great general management program in one of the best towns there is. Though it's got a high-ish admit rate, it does better in the overall rankings and has a better national brand than the others in the same range. Ross sent 36% of its most recent class into Consulting, 21.4% into Finance, 21% into Marketing. Keep post-grad geography in mind, as 38% go to work in the Midwest, 23.4% West and 20% to Northeast.

- ★ Can't Miss Class: Commuter Logistics 401: Finding Parking in 3-feet of Snow
- ★ Strengths: Ann Arbor is a killer town. Worth living there even if you don't want an MBA. Go Big Blue!
- ★ Weaknesses: The post-grad likelihood of working in Detroit

Yale School of Management

Founded in 1976, Yale SOM is a veritable infant among much longer-established programs. But as part of 315-year-old Yale, it doesn't feel like a newcomer. Though it has a reputation as a bit of a hippy school, SOM boasts a healthy median GMAT of 720 and sent 25% of recent grads into Finance of one flavor or another.

Twenty-six percent head into consulting with the balance pursuing careers in a relatively diverse collection of industries. Almost 8% of SOM grads go into non-profit or government and over 6% accept jobs in the energy sector. Evans Hall, a much needed 214,000 square foot headquarters, opened in 2014. It provides a working and social space that is "informed in the past, work(ing) in the present," which is also a good description of Yale SOM itself.

★ Study group: Collegial. Hard-working

★ Quirk: "Strong in non-profit management and finance. Two different types of people at same school"

★ Opportunities: "New Building, New dean--sky's the limit"

★ Strengths: Collaborative, Non-profit, Finance, Non-traditional students

University of North Carolina Kenan-Flagler Business School

With 276 in the in-coming class, KFBS is on the smaller side, but one hears a lot about the power and warmth of the school community. Academic work is heavy on case studies and group work. Marketing, consulting and finance functions each claimed about a quarter of the Class of '14. A large portion (38%) stuck around the South, but 14% headed to the Northeast, 16% to the West and the rest scattered themselves about Mid-Atlantic, Midwest, Southwest and international destinations.

★ Strengths: Chapel Hill is simply delightful. Ahhhhhhh

★ Strengths 2: If you happen to live in North Carolina, KFBS provides you the tastiest in-state tuition discounts (~27%+) of any of the leading schools

★ Weaknesses: Not the most diverse school on the planet

★ Quirk: UNCKF is the most logical acronym for this school, but it is rarely used, for reasons you'll discover when you unscramble the letters

Samuel Curtis Johnson Graduate School of Management at Cornell University

Amidst upstate New York's Finger Lakes district thrives Cornell's Johnson School. A full semester "hands-on" learning immersion program distinguishes Johnson from other top schools. During the back half of the first year, students choose to dive into one of the following areas: Capital Markets, Digital Technology, Investment Banking, Managerial Finance, Operations, Marketing or Sustainable Global Enterprise. Johnson also offers a unique Consulting Program, custom-made for students who are totally jacked-up to join the thriving industry. Cornell's campus is awesome and Ithaca is beautiful. Students bond in the snow before 38% of them head off to careers in finance.

★ Quirk: The longest official name of any top program, "Samuel Curtis Johnson Graduate School of Management at Cornell University" makes "The University of Texas at Austin McCombs School of Business" sound like an abbreviation. Also the only program whose name includes "Curtis."

★ Strengths: Dining scene in Ithaca is surprisingly awesome.

The University of Texas at Austin McCombs School of Business

I am jealous that you even get to consider two fun years (and potentially many more) in Austin. Cohort-based McCombs is strong in accounting/finance, energy and high tech, and sends a quarter of its grads into consulting. Those interested in venture capital and entrepreneurship also have much to choose from here. McCombs doesn't have the giant national footprint of some of the other top schools, but it is a very strong program with tremendous credibility. As one alum put it, "If you want to land in Texas, McCombs is the gold standard."

* Strengths 1: Austin culture: an unbelievable music scene. Great food. Mad Dog Margaritas at The Chili Parlor. Shiner Bock. Handsome, rugged dudes. Drop-dead gorgeous, whip-smart women. Hell, why didn't I go here?

* Strengths 2: Austin business scene: there is a ton of professional opportunity in Austin, especially in technology and venture capital.

* Opportunities: Growing the McCombs brand nationally. Sixty-four percent of the Class of '14 went to work in the Southwest, with only 17% in the West and 5% each in the Northeast and Midwest.

* Quirk: You get to do that "Hook-em-horns" thing with your fingers for the rest of your life!

Vanderbilt Owen School of Management

Owen is a very strong brand in the Southern U.S., and continues to bolster its national competiveness. Over the past 5 years, Owen has raised its average GMAT by 15 points (to 688), a number that rivals many higher-ranked schools. The school is nestled in the heart of Nashville, a cool town that alumni describe as "STRONG" (all-caps theirs) and claim to be cooler than Austin. That is a bold assertion, but demonstrates some major fan loyalty. Intense studying at Owen Sunday through Thursday afternoon transitions into lots of fun Thursday night through the weekend. Alumni are accessible and helpful.

* Strengths: Healthcare and HR programs. The Owen community, which is described as an "absolutely, amazing group of people who worked together for self improvement."

* Weaknesses: The never-ending fight to crack the top of the national rankings.
* Quirk: Owen's first location was in a former funeral home. Also, that Vanderbilt Commodore guy is creepy looking.

Emory University Goizueta Business School

Named for Roberto Goizueta, the former CEO/Chairman of the Coca-Cola Company, Goizueta joins Owen as one of the top two business school brands in the South. As such, it hosts both a strong full-time program but also vibrant executive and part-time MBA tracks. The full-time two-year program is a tight 166 students, with a 5:1 student/faculty ratio. Goizueta ranks very high in job placement, sending its grads into Consulting (38%), Marketing (23%) and Finance (19%), with 62% remaining in the South.

* Quirk: Coke-centric. "No matter...what cases we studied, it all went back to Coca-Cola. Traditional brand management at its finest."
* Strengths: In Atlanta. A "brand name down the street." Collaboration. In study groups "it was understood who would do the reading, who would teach the rest of the group, who got the concepts quicker, who brought the beer, who was useless, etc."
* Weaknesses: Surrounded by Georgia. Pleated khakis.

Tepper School of Business, Carnegie-Mellon University

At 200 students per class, Tepper is on the smaller side, but the school rocks a mighty analytical punch. A faculty that has produced nine Nobel Laureates teaches full-time MBA'ers (50% of whom majored in science and engineering in undergrad) to master leadership and analytics. After completing the mandatory first-year core classes, students have the opportunity to dive into CMU's other rigorous academic departments and take classes in computer science, robotics, design, engineering and more. Tepper has just broken ground on expanded facilities called the Tepper Quad, named for alumnus and hedge fund stud David Tepper. Tepper sent 27% of the most recent grads into consulting, 16% into financial services, 33% into technology, 8% pharma/biotech/healthcare.

★ 9% Minorities, 35% international, 687 Average GMAT.

★ Weakness: With only 29% women, you might not find your wife at Tepper. But if you do, she'll be reeeel smart.

★ Summing up the Tepper product: "Our students excel at strategic thinking, executive communication, competitive presentations, high-stakes negotiations and conflict resolution. Tepper School MBAs are highly sought after for their strategic abilities in analytical frameworks and complex decision-making."

Indiana University—Kelley School of Business

With a class size just under 200, Kelley offers a real focus on the student. A committed, enthusiastic faculty teaches one of the most integrated curricula of any top school. Kelley fuses this solid, customizable academic experience with a unique emphasis on personal discovery, offering students a massive amount of coaching and the opportunity to develop "an in-depth understanding of yourself" through Me, Inc., one of the hallmarks of the Kelley MBA experience. Me, Inc. helps connect students' strengths, interests and experiences to future career success via mentoring, networking and advice. It may sound like they're coddling the student, but the process exists so that Kelley can help students "Take ownership of (their) career path" through Kelley's formula of Discovery, Networking, Interviewing, and Performing. They must be doing something right, as recent classes have seen near or at 100% employment 3 months after graduation!

* Geography: 56% of Graduates stick around the Midwest after graduation.
* Industries: Kelley sends the usual large chunk of its graduates to both consulting and financial services, but also a notable 27.5% into marketing and sales. Finally—a top MBA program that understands how important sales people are!

USC Marshall School of Business

Located in the heart of LA, Marshall is a smaller program (222 in latest class) that emphasizes entrepreneurship and global outreach, especially to the Pacific Rim. After completing the core requirements, Marshall students choose from over 100 electives to round out their degree requirements. The school is strengthening its resources, offerings and brand through a $400 million capital campaign, which will be used for scholarships, new facilities and programming. Being in LA offers students access to the best of Southern California's dynamic lifestyle and corporate dynamism. New graduates land jobs in consulting (20%), technology (17%), consumer products (9%), financial service (12%) and media/entertainment (5%).

* Strengths: The Trojan Family. Marshall's small classes forge strong ties to the institution.
* Weakness: Traffic. One alum advises those who have early classes, "Consider sleeping in your car."
* Median GMAT: 690.
* Alumni include a director at the Jet Propulsion Lab, the founder of Kinko's, the co-founder of Pinkberry and Chris DeWolfe, former CEO of MySpace who has been romantically linked to Paris Hilton. Marshall makes no

claims that they will help you land a celebutante girlfriend, but you've clearly got a better chance landing one in LA than you do in, say, Pittsburgh (no offense, Tepper).

★ Geography: A high concentration (86%) of new graduates took jobs in the U.S. West, but they're going to some great companies like Apple, Amgen, Goldman, GE, DirecTV.

Georgetown University McDonough School of Business

You can't really talk about McDonough without talking about its location. Set on the banks of the Potomac River, Georgetown University has a beautiful and historic campus in one of the coolest neighborhoods of Washington D.C. Then there is D.C. itself. The U.S. capital provides a dynamic environment and a host of opportunities for McDonough's students who come from over 45 countries across the globe. Speaking of the globe, McDonough strives to be a leader in the international business field, with the Global Business Experience program's goal of providing all students with an international consulting project before graduation. McDonough's tight-knit class has over 40 student organizations to choose from, including the Beer Appreciation Society, Georgetown Gourmet Society, Georgetown Wine Society, MBA Golf Club and a whole bunch that are about business too. Top employers who seek out McDonough grads include Amazon, American Express, Citi, BofA and (of course) consulting firms like Deloitte, E&Y, KPMG and PWC.

★ Strengths: Washington D.C. and all its amenities, including potential employers like the FBI!

Washington University in St. Louis—Olin Business School

With an average GMAT just shy of 700 and an acceptance rate of 26.7%, Olin rocks numbers competitive with many much higher-ranked schools. This is not a complete surprise when you consider that Olin also offers MS degrees in Accounting, Finance (Corporate or Quantitative,) Supply Chain Management or Customer Analytics, i.e. programs that are going to pull in some hardcore students. Like Kelley, Olin places meaningful emphasis on career preparedness. ProDev is a required career education program that all students start on day one of their first year. Students also select a Career Platform (in either Consulting, Corporate Finance & Investments, Entrepreneurship, Marketing or Operations & Supply Chain Management), then dive deep to build knowledge, contacts and job prospects in their chosen field. The results seem to speak for themselves: Olin's 3-moth post-graduation employment rate has increased from 91% for the class of 2009 to a stellar 97% for the class of 2014. Olin sent 31% of its last class into a marketing/sales function, and about 16-18% to pursue jobs doing consulting, financial services and general management. Fifty-eight percent ended up in the Midwest, with about 10% in both the South and the Southwest (not including California).

★ Size: Olin hosts a petite class of 140.

★ A Family Tradition: The school is named for John Olin, the son of Frank Olin, an industrialist who made a fortune in the munitions business and whose foundation funded many schools, including F.W. Olin Graduate School of Business at Babson.

CHAPTER 10

THE GMAT

I F YOU WANT TO GO TO BUSINESS SCHOOL, YOU'RE GOING TO have to prove that you can read and do a little math.

That's reasonable, right?

Sure, your college transcript may tell that story for you, but the quality and rigor of college curricula vary greatly, so AdComs need a universal metric by which to ensure that potential admits can get through a Dr. Seuss book and calculate a tip.

Enter the Graduate Management Admissions Test, or GMAT, the standardized test used to provide a level-playing-field benchmark for the MBA applicant.

FUN FACT!

GMAC (Graduate Management Admissions Council) is the name of the organization that administers the GMAT. GMAC is also the name of a hip-hop artist whose rap song *Turnt UP* begins:

"I'm addicted to the money...if it ain't about them hundreds, <expletive>, you ain't sayin' nothing."

Coincidence?

Note: many business schools also accept the GRE, another standardized test for graduate school admission, but taking the GRE is basically cheating (see the GMAT v. GRE box, which is coming up in a few pages).

Going all "Method" on the GMAT

Most people applying to business school have to navigate the GMAT. And as—in the writing of this book—I have tried to put myself back into the mindset of the business school applicant, I needed to re-familiarize myself with this very important step in the application process.

So I went online, found and started taking some GMAT practice tests. Cold.

Yikes.

The first thing I learned was that the GMAT has changed a lot since I took it in 1994 (more on that below).

The next thing I learned was that these practice tests were kicking my ass. They were most difficult. Like, math-in-a-foreign-tongue difficult (which the GMAT actually *is* for many who take it).

Speaking of foreign, there's no partial credit on the GMAT… and that's just un-American.

Unfortunately, the "in English" parts of the test weren't easy either.

The more online practice tests I took, the more clear it became that I didn't remember the Pythagorean Theorem, how to compute the area of a trapezoid or how to correct sentences real good.

"Boy, to do well on this test, one's really got to study hard!" I thought. "That's a lot of pressure."

And if studying for and taking the GMAT is part of the b-school application process, then it must be a part of writing this book.

So in 2015 I registered to take the GMAT for my second time. And I started studying again…for real.

The best way I can tell you about the experience is to share my diary entries:

Re-taking the GMAT, 21 Years Later (*from Paul's Journal*)

Here I am in suburban Atlanta at the Pearson test center, where in 30 minutes I will be taking the GMAT, the test that will determine which business schools will find me to be an attractive candidate.

It's going to be a four-hour grind requiring focus, efficiency and mental endurance. To maintain my mental acuity I have brought a bottle of water and a Nature Valley granola bar, which I'll consume during my brief intra-test break.

My heart is racing. My hands are clammy. I am more than a little nauseous.

I really shouldn't be this nervous. I've studied. I've reviewed. I've taken multiple practice tests.

But the main reason I shouldn't be nervous is that I already have an MBA.

I check in. Dude behind the desk asks my name, reviews my ID, then scans my palm for vein-patterning identification. CIA technology to deter cheaters. All right, GMAC.

I return to the waiting area to realize that I can't find my granola bar. This is not okay. I'm not a diabetic or anything—I just get really whiny when I'm hungry.

I go back to the desk and ask, "Did you see the granola bar I left up here?"

"Uhhh, no," he replies, offering a cursory glance around his desk, then looking at me like I'm a deranged idiot.

"It's Oats 'n Honey," I add, confirming his suspicion.

Dude couldn't care less.

Does this guy know what's at stake here? This is game day! This is the Super Bowl that determines whether I have the goods to pretend apply to HBS or Stanford! If this were my first crack at the test, I would be freaking out.

But it's not.

I first took the GMAT on Saturday, June 18, 1994. I was 25 years old, and hungry in my soul to take my career to the next level.

The test date is notable for two reasons: #1—the evening prior, O.J. Simpson led scores of police on a televised chase around Los Angeles (thus making last minute studying impossible) and #2—it was one of the last GMATs that included only the verbal and quant sections.

Shortly after that test, GMAC decided MBAs should be able to write more than just lunch orders and "You're fired!" memos. So they added what is now the Analytical Writing Assessment.

A few years after that they added the Integrated Reasoning section. And now it's all jacked up. *Author's note: reasoning doesn't seem to have totally "caught on" in the business world.*

So to prepare for this second test, I had both a lot to review and a lot of new concepts to learn.

I bought *The Official Guide for GMAT 2015*. I cracked the 838 page, 4 pound tome. The font was small—so small I could barely read it. This was the first of many red flags.

I perused the first practice exam. The math was unrecognizable. This was of particular concern because the quant section was my strength on my last GMAT. Back then I was only seven years removed from high school, so recalling secondary math rules was much easier than it is today.

At 46, knowledge of geometry isn't recalled so much as it is exhumed. I have to jackhammer through the asphalt of time and dust away decades of dirt to remember that the area of a polygon = 180(*n*-2) where *n* = awww hell man, my life is halfway over and nobody is EVER going to ask me this stuff again before I die!

It's not that knowing how to compute the area of a trapezoid has zero value to humankind, but one is unlikely to ever hear the following in a job interview:

"We really like you and we love the way you think about the marketplace. So we're going to make you a very generous offer… right after you tell us the area of this mutant rectangle."

Compounding my frustration with the apparent pointlessness of the questions was the fact that the practice test was legitimately hard. It felt like a young person's game.

My brain felt like it was in the same shape as my middle-aged body. Which means that my frontal lobe is balding and my cerebellum sports man-boobs and a muffin-top. Perhaps it's natural atrophy, but it couldn't have been helped by 15 years of trans-scalp Rogaine absorption.

So, the modern GMAT quant section is much harder than what I remembered. And these new sections aren't much fun either.

This is all on my mind as I begin my official test. Here we go.

The writing portion proves to be more annoying than hard. It seems to exist as a hurdle for international students to prove their English fluency. Still, it's 30 minutes of pass/fail distraction that absorbs my very finite mental energy.

The quantitative section goes very much as described above, but I think I did okay. I'm not sure about those data sufficiency answers.

The reading comprehension stuff is stressful, but mainly makes me grateful that English is my first language.

The Integrated Reasoning section, on the other hand, is a mind-bending pain in the ass—like taking the SAT on peyote. It seems to exist only to screw with my head and make me doubt myself. The obvious answer to *every* question is "Who gives a shit?" but I don't see that listed among my choices.

"Haha. I'm funny," I think to myself and begin to repeat this rhetorical mantra.

Then something dawns on me: that's actually why the GMAT is here—to find out who gives a shit and who doesn't.

Yes, its primary purpose is to determine whether one can read and do math. But beyond that, it's a litmus test of commitment to the business school application game itself.

And while this game has plenty of other elements that can be humorously poked and prodded, it is a well-honed process that effectively evaluates not just the taker's brainage, but also the degree of his hunger, which is at least as important to one's long-term success.

"Perhaps there was an easier way to come to this realization than putting myself through this exercise," I think to myself. But it doesn't matter now, as I am already done with my test. I let out a long breath.

So here we are.

Before they show me the score, they ask if I want this score to count. Yes I do. Because unless I lose a very stupid bet in the future, I will not be taking this freaking test again.

Do I want to see my score now? Yes I do (drumroll, please):

* **640**
* **71st percentile**

Uggh. I am not happy. With this score, Harvard and Stanford won't pretend recruit me. Nor will my beloved alma mater… despite the fact that I am a meta-legacy.

I am disappointed, as I had done much better on practice tests. Damn you, data sufficiency questions!

But really, what could I expect? I studied for maybe 10 hours. If there's anything my score reflects it's that I don't give enough of a shit about the test itself.

What I do give a shit about, however, is examining the connection between humor and business wherever it exists. I am fascinated by the game, the language and the players. I am fascinated by what people—myself included—do to succeed.

So in that context, this has been a very useful exercise. But, come on—640?

Perhaps I still have the intellectual firepower to score higher on the GMAT. But clearly my dilettante test prep can't compete against those who actually give a shit. Clearly I have not committed myself to the process.

Clearly I am not sufficiently hungry. Despite having lost my granola bar.

Here is a useful chart to find out if you give enough of a shit...

GMAT Score	IMPLICATIONS
800	You are a genius. You don't need an MBA. Go do something worthwhile with your life.
750 - 799	You are going to a top school, unless you have a criminal record (or even if you do).
700 - 749	You're in the zone. It's no slam-dunk, but you are super-admittable.
650 - 699	You're not setting any records here, but you can still get in to a very decent program with this score.
600 - 649	Meh. Take the test again.
550 - 599	Do you have any friends on the AdCom? You're going to need them because this isn't a good score. It's not even "good-adjacent."
500 - 549	You might be super-nice, but you're not super-smart. Look on the bright side—the MBA program that finds you to be an attractive candidate will likely have an excellent football team.
400 - 499	How much cough syrup did you drink before taking the test? You could have played Candy Crush for four hours and still scored higher than this. Give up.
300 - 399	You are a houseplant. I hope your owner doesn't forget to water you.
200 - 299	You had points deducted for misspelling your name, and you missed every single question thereafter.

GMAT V. GRE

As an alternative to taking the GMAT, one can also take the GRE, a standardized test that can also be used for admission into many other (non-business) graduate programs.

THERE ARE SOME ADVANTAGES TO TAKING THE GRE:

1. The GRE contains no Integrated Reasoning questions (these suck, so they are worth avoiding).

2. The Math section is reported to be much easier than the GMAT's.

THERE CAN BE SOME DRAWBACKS TO TAKING THE GRE:

1. As the GRE can be used for more than just business schools, some AdComs may interpret a GRE score as a sign that the applicant is hedging on her commitment to business school (presumably there are thousands of applicants giving equal consideration to a career on Wall Street or a career in linguistic anthropology).

2. Some AdComs may interpret one taking the GRE as a sign that one can't do math. They might not be wrong.

Call me overly traditional and biased toward what we did in the old days, but the way I see it is if you don't take the GMAT, you're basically cheating. Because if I had to take it, you should have to take it too.

Further, if you don't take the GMAT, you're just not putting yourself through the whole, legitimate, complete torture of the business school application experience. To paraphrase comedian and *Saturday Night Live* alumnus, Kevin Nealon, "It's like going to Las Vegas and not getting a hooker."

Then again, your goal here is to get into a great program, not to be a hero. And a recent Kaplan survey indicated that 8 out of 10 business schools had no test preference between the GMAT and the GRE.

So what the hell do I know? Follow your heart.

CHAPTER 11

THE
APPLICATION
PROCESS

W HO THE HELL ARE YOU AND WHAT WILL YOU BRING TO our program?

That is the essential question schools are trying to answer during the application process.

Consisting mostly of an interview and a small number of personal essays, the application process is a weed-out round that forces the applicant to articulate who he is, why he wants to go to business school, what role it will play in his life and beyond the ivy walls. Just like the GMAT, it is a process designed to figure out who gives a shit.

You must therefore dive into the process and bare your soul, or at least the best parts thereof. It will be challenging, cathartic and maddening at times.

Recall the rhetorical questions I asked you to consider back in Chapter 3:

- What do you want to do with you life? Really, like, what's your dream? If you could do anything, what would it be?

- Why does getting an MBA help you achieve that goal?

- Why do you want to go to the individual school you're talking to? Like, what things about that program make it a better fit for you and your dreams?

Now's the time to dust off the answers you wrote down and start turning them into a cogent, thoughtful, funny, moving and persuasive argument for your candidacy.

Essays: Why they have to be great

First, remember the "competition": I know, I know—one shouldn't consider fellow b-school applicants "the competition." But recall that at Harvard and Stanford, there are about 10 applicants for every seat. And that even well down the list into the top 25 programs there are still 4 applicants for every possible admission. So given the finite number of positions in the incoming class of any top school, the admissions process *is indeed* a competition, which makes all those other applicants…well, you get it.

And these other applicants are good. They're not directionless stoners who are so bored they decided to apply to business school. They are similarly motivated, ambitious, career-minded people like you. People who made great grades at great schools…or at least good grades at good schools.

So suffice to say—the competition for admission is intense.

Second, consider your audience: the AdCom members who will be reading your essays. While all these great schools take great care to give each application individual consideration, the sheer number of applicants must make the task overwhelming at some point.

It all happens electronically now, but I remember seeing the Tuck admissions officers sitting in the library with stacks (plural) of printed applications, each seven or eight inches high. Assuming there were only 10 applications in each stack, and each application contained 3 essays, that's 30 essays per stack times 2 stacks, or 60 essays that said officer was reading *that day.*

So you as an applicant must find a way to stand out among the other smart, motivated people who are applying for admission. To do that, you must move that overwhelmed reader with honesty, emotion, humor or biting clarity in a way she has not been moved by the other 56 essays she's reading.

Essay Lesson: Financial Semantics— It's Not About the Money (Yes it is)

The most important thing you have to demonstrate in the business school application and interview process is your ability to talk about money as if it is incidental to your interest in advancing your career via obtaining an MBA.

Rule Number One of talking about money is to pretend that you're not talking about money even while everyone knows that money is the only thing you're talking about. It's just like not talking about sex with someone while they're deciding if they're going to sleep with you.

What you do is talk about money in code. It is a requirement of polite adult society, and you must show the admissions committee that you either already know how to do this or that you are ready to learn how.

Admission folk test for this by asking you over and over again— in a hundred different ways—why you want to go to business school. In so doing, they are almost inviting you to blurt out crassly "I HAVE TO EARN $10MM TO MAKE MY EX-GIRLFRIEND REGRET DUMPING ME!!!!"

At which point your interviewer will make some important notes on your file.

So while your answer may clearly be that you want to make a lot of money, you cannot come right out and say so.

It's totally fine that you want to rake in a pile of cash (who doesn't?). What's more, your business school *totally* wants you to make a fortune. After all, having filthy rich alumni brings the school prestige and shiny new buildings.

But they would NEVER come right out and say it. And neither can you. It's a "wink-wink/nudge-nudge" kind of game that is not logical. So this chapter is here to help you see how to play it.

First, let's look at the concept in practice:

TECH 9/15/2014 @ 11:23AM | 7,624 views

'Minecraft' Creator On $2.5 Billion Deal: 'It's Not About The Money'

Zuckerberg: It's Not Always About the Money

January 14, 2015, 3:31 PM PST

Billionaire financier tells judge: 'I don't care about money'

After Hillary claims the Clintons aren't 'really rich' Chelsea (who's married to a hedge funder, lives in a $11m home, and is paid $600,000 for doing nothing) says 'I tried to care about money but I couldn't'

At Davos, it's not all about the money...seriously

See what I mean? This is the "money talk" game as played by monetary Zen masters with net-worths approaching the infinite. Notice how it's rich people who don't care about money. Ironic, eh? You bust your ass for your entire life to try to get rich. Then when you get rich, you pretend like you don't care. That's messed up.

Now consider this:

"When somebody says it's not about the money,
it's about the money."
—*H.L. Mencken*

Okay, so it IS about the money? Of course it is! But you have to pretend that it's not. It's sick and twisted, but that's the way the game is played. And the admissions committee wants to know that you'll be able to play that game when your time comes.

Am I being cynical here? Yeah, a little. But I'm not wrong.

Here's a guide of how you say one thing about money but mean something completely different:

WHAT YOU SAY IN YOUR APPLICATION	WHAT IT MEANS
It's not about the money.	It so clearly *is* about the money.

This is entry-level, 101 money talk. But you win points here by acknowledging the elephant in the room. What you're saying here is, "Hey MBA AdCom, I know this is a game we're playing. And I'm down. I'm not going to be the gauche jerk who talks only about money when I'm interviewing for full-time gigs during my second year. And I'm going to make the school look good when I get rich. Because it's not about the money (insert "winky-eyed" emoticon here)."

WHAT YOU SAY IN YOUR APPLICATION	WHAT IT MEANS
I want to build something.	...so I can make more money.

"Build" is a really good word. It evokes progress and community and whole lot of other positive things. But what it tells them (in code!) is that you are ambitious and want to run something, have people work for you and earn margin on the finite hours of their lives that they dedicate to whatever the hell you are building.

God bless you, builder of something!

WHAT YOU SAY IN YOUR APPLICATION	WHAT IT MEANS
I have a unique talent that I want to develop.	...and use it to make a lot of money.

Okay, great. This tells them two things: 1. You're special/have something to offer the school, and 2. You know how to talk around the issue of wanting to collect a heaping cornucopia of cash. You are on the right path.

WHAT YOU SAY IN YOUR APPLICATION	WHAT IT MEANS
I want to disrupt market inefficiencies.	...and, in the process, make an unfathomable amount of money.

Yes. Yes. Yes! This kid throws the long-ball / swings for the fences. Every school needs a number of these kinds of financial demigods. Whether it's toppling the currency of a small Asian nation or using proprietary (and probably illegal) software to capture micro-points to the tunes of billions of dollars, "disrupting inefficiencies" is code for "millions is not nearly enough for me!" If they think you've got a 1-in-1,000 chance of pulling it off, they'll let you in.

Note: you're going to have to augment this with a whole bunch of frou-frou community leadership stuff that tells them what they want to hear about you being "a complete, well-rounded person." Whatever.

WHAT YOU SAY IN YOUR APPLICATION	WHAT IT MEANS
I'm not after money for money's sake.	No, that'd be far too prosaic. I'm after money because it's a means of measuring human worth. When I amass way more than other people, it means I defeat them in a barely-civilized caveman game of Survival of the Greediest. I'm the winner.

You have risen to a whole other level. The Machiavellian subtext signals that you are a cold-hearted killer but one with enough charm and grace to smile at your victim while you choke the last breath out of their confused, middle-class face. You belong at Wharton (or Harvard).

Money Glossary

Just like the business school population, moneyed-people have their own language. To talk about money like you already have it, you have to learn the code.

The first step is to learn the ways to say "money" without actually saying "money." I don't mean crass street lingo for money like "paper," "cabbage" or "Benjamins." I mean boardroom and country club bar terms that mean money. You'll be using these terms for the rest of your career. Whether negotiating a pay package, or signaling politely (but quite clearly) to a potential mate that you have a lot of, ahem, resources.

Use these in your essays and interviews, and you brand yourself as an applicant who is already ready for the post-MBA world.

ALTERNATIVE WORD	WHAT IT MEANS
Resources	Money
Capital	Money
Assets	Money
Property	Money
Means	Money
Shares	Money
Wherewithal	Money
Endowment	Penis*

*Or "money." But more likely "penis." (In many ways these are synonyms.)

Some Essay Question Examples

Most schools are going to have a collection of questions that look very similar. They are there to give them an idea of:

- Who are you?
- Why do you want to come to this particular school?
- What are your professional aspirations?

- What are you going to contribute to our program and community?
- Tell us about a leadership experience or how you have overcome adversity in your life/career.
- Etc.

These are all pretty straightforward, and provide you with the open door to tell the school what you want to tell them about yourself. Of course some schools make it a little more interesting… which doesn't necessarily make it any easier.

Harvard has one essay. It sets the scene that it is the very first day of school. That the applicant is in his new, 90-person HBS section, and that these section mates will forge life-lasting, career-making bonds.

Then Harvard says, "Introduce yourself."

Intimidated? I damn near pissed myself when I read that, and I'm not even applying.

Stanford asks the crazy wide-open question, "What matters most to you and why?"

That's it.

"Wait, what? Aren't you going to give me any more specific direction, Stanford? *I need guidelines!*"

"Nope," replies Stanford. "Good luck, kid."

Other schools get even more creative.

Stern requests of applicants, "Please describe yourself to your MBA classmates. You may use almost any method to convey your message (e.g. words, illustrations). Feel free to be creative." They then go on to say, "Do not submit anything perishable (e.g. food)…"

This begs the natural question: what kind of off-the-wall nonsense have applicants submitted in the past? "Hello, classmates, please find enclosed a half-eaten, insect-covered guava that represents my metamorphosis from childhood to adulthood."

Haas asks the brilliant question "If you could choose one song that expresses who you are, what is it and why?"

This opens up all kinds of doors to express insight, creativity and passion (if also to the pitfalls of kitsch and cliché). No matter how well you can articulate your passion, your chosen song should not be anything by Ke$ha and definitely shouldn't be "Wait" by the Ying Yang Twins (if you're not familiar with it, you probably don't want to Google it).

Fuqua asks applicants to list 25 Random Things about themselves. This must yield some crazy freaking answers... See the box below for some the kinds of self-revelations that should not be included.

---

15 SELF-REVELATIONS TO NOT INCLUDE IN FUQUA'S "25 RANDOM THINGS ABOUT YOU" ESSAY

1. I am assertive. If I see something I want, I take it.

2. I once ate 5 Cinnabons in a 24-hour period. When a friend asked me why I did it, I told her, "Because I'm awesome."

3. When I travel on a commercial airplane, I approach the experience through the lens of zero-sum Darwinism.

4. My son recently suggested that I lack the moral authority to enforce our house-wide ban on nose-picking.

5. I believe in getting things right the first time. One of my direct reports once sent me an Excel spreadsheet that wasn't formatted properly for printing. I punched him in the throat and smashed his laptop. (He hasn't done it again.)

6. I once went three weeks without showering or using deodorant. I wasn't hiking the Appalachian Trail or anything. I just didn't feel like cleaning myself.

7. In college, when I learned a devastating hurricane had displaced thousands of poor people in Louisiana, I took up a collection from my fellow students. I then took that money

---

and bought oil futures, which spiked immediately. I dumped my position, returned the principle to my classmates and pocketed the proceeds. If it weren't for Hurricane Katrina, I wouldn't have been able to afford a new snowboard or tickets to Coachella!

8. I thoroughly enjoy the occasional Vicodin washed down with a goblet or two of yummy merlot.

9. Even though I'm almost 27, I have chosen to continue living in my parents' basement because it allows me to be close to my extensive collection of *Star Trek* memorabilia.

10. I just don't have the time to recycle.

11. In high school I dated a boy who looked a little bit like Yoda. He wasn't a Jedi and he didn't do the inverse subject/ predicate thing when he talked, but there was definitely some Yoda energy happening there. And I dug it.

12. If there is a margin call in the next month, there's a very good chance I will be going to jail.

13. Conformity is a concept that has served me very well in pursuing the upper middle-class dream. I teach my kids that it is a good idea to be just like everyone else.

14. If I could have any super power, it would be the ability to avoid paying taxes.

15. A census-taker once tried to test me. I ate his liver with some fava beans and a nice chianti.

Recommendations

As part of the application process, schools require a recommendation from someone(s) who have worked closely with you.

These recommenders will answer lengthy questions about your strengths and weaknesses and give you an overall rating, e.g.

"Definitely admit this person," "Probably admit this person" or "Run Like Hell!" Be sure to pick someone who knows you well, and believes in you. A good recommendation takes time to prepare, and a sub-par recommendation can torpedo your whole application.

While there are some guidelines to adhere to, your essays and recommendations give you plenty of leeway to position the YOU product (your history, your ambitions, your reasoning for choosing said school). If these elements tell a complete, consistent and interesting story of a candidate that any school would love to admit, you'll get the chance to interview (that is, assuming your test scores and college GPA pass muster).

Speaking of your interviews...

The Interview

Congratulations! At many top schools, an invitation to interview means that you've made the first cut. You will thus have the privilege of discussing your candidacy with an admissions staffer, alum or a second year student.

This is where the school puts a face with the name on the application. It's your time to shine, if you do the prep work. Here is a non-exhaustive list of things to keep in mind:

- **Be consistent.** You're going to be asked again, "Why MBA?" and "Why here?" In the back of your big brain you might be thinking, "Please...I am so tired of answering that questions. I promise I'm smart and will work hard. PLEASE just let me in." Unfortunately, that answer is considered—as MBAs would say—"sub-optimal."

- So you're going to need to stay on course here on the homestretch. Do a gut check—are you telling the same story in your interview as you are in your application? For example, if you said your post-graduate plans were to trade derivatives on Wall Street, don't use your interview to discuss your dream to launch a line of vegan pet food.

- **Do your research** about the school's interviewing technique. Fuqua and Tuck are more likely to feel like friendly conversations, whereas Sloan has a whole framework for their interviews, the Behavioral Event-based Interview…which sounds pretty damn intense. Wharton's format is called TBD, for Team-Based Discussion wherein the applicant works to solve a problem with four to five other applicants (i.e. the competition!). If it sounds vaguely like *The Hunger Games*, that's not a coincidence. This is Wharton, people! May the odds be ever in your favor.

- **Know the school** and be prepared for what they are likely to ask you and how they will conduct the interview (see Sloan and Wharton examples above). Harvard is going to ask you about leadership. Kellogg is going to ask you about teamwork. You'll need to cite examples of these attributes in your career so far. They should be specific and impressive but presented with humility. Demonstrate your knowledge of and enthusiasm for the school. If asked, give them several examples of why you are excited to go there and how you will contribute to their vibrant community.

- **Know yourself.** Anything that is on your resume or mentioned in your written application is fair game. Know it cold, and know why it's there. For example, why did you choose your college? How did you pick your first job? Why do you insist on using **16 point sans serif font?**

- **Smile.** Even if you're geared up to knock the Booth or Sloan interviewer out with your crazy analytical intellect, work in a sincere chuckle or two. Business schools are looking for positive, enthusiastic people who will make their programs more enjoyable. Show them that you are a fun, optimistic person with infectious energy. Or just, you know, do your best to smile.

DO SAY/DON'T SAY GUIDELINES FOR YOUR B-SCHOOL INTERVIEW	
Do Say	Don't Say
"I'm looking to move away from finance into a senior operational role."	"I can't run with the big dogs on Wall Street."
"My extensive undergraduate extracurricular activities sometimes interfered with top academic performance."	"I did, like, SO MANY drugs in college."
"I'm not a good test-taker."	"I bombed the GMAT 'cuz I'm dumb."
"It's really important to me that the program I attend embraces strong ethical principles and inclusiveness."	"I'll say whatever it takes to get in."
"I am a fiscal conservative and social progressive."	"I am a greedy pervert."
"While my post-business school career plans are evolving…"	"I have no earthly idea what I want to do with my MBA, but anything is better than what I'm doing now!"

The Waiting is the Hardest Part

You've gone through the exploration process. You've talked to friends, done your research. You've studied for and slayed the GMAT. You've visited campuses, written essays and wowed interviewers with your commitment to invigorate your career with an MBA-injection.

Researching and applying for the MBA has been a life-defining experience for the past year. You have spent more time working toward MBA program admission than doing anything else except your job. Perhaps even more than your job.

You've busted your ass and done all you can to present your brilliant self brilliantly to these schools.

Now you wait.

You wait for that phone call. That e-mail. That date when you check the school website to learn the fate of your application.

You wait for those AdComs to judge the quality of the image of your life that you have put before them. It is stressful. You have so much invested in the process and have begun to define your future plans through the presumption—or at very least the hope—that you will be attending an excellent school next fall.

It's no fun.

Maybe you get into your dream school. Maybe you have to settle for a fall-back or get wait-listed. Maybe you don't get into any of the schools you applied to, and have to re-evaluate going through the whole process again one year from now. Uggh. That would suck.

But take heart, dear applicant. No matter the outcome, the world will keep spinning. And if this is something you really want, you will find a way to make it happen, one way or another.

I'm crossing my fingers for you. If all else fails—or even if it succeeds—you can always become a comedian.

EPILOGUE

NOBODY CARES
ABOUT YOUR
MBA

WHAT MORE INSPIRING TITLE COULD YOU ASK FOR AT THE end of a book about the grueling exercise of getting an MBA, huh?

After all the pain and turmoil you've been through (or that lies ahead of you) in this process, you get to the end only to be told it doesn't matter.

Wow.

"Wait one darn second, Paul—weren't you the one who told me in Chapter 1 that the MBA would win me the respect of strangers and free Diet Sprites on airplanes?"

Yes, I was.

"And now you say that the MBA doesn't matter. What gives?"

Hey, hey, pipe down—I didn't say that the MBA doesn't matter. I believe it matters a great deal.

To you.

What I said just now was that nobody else cares about it. I did so just to share the perspective that relatively few other human beings will find it as important as you do.

Yes, your parents and spouse will be proud of you, and you will be proud of yourself. As you should be. Further, your first—and maybe second—employer out of school will probably place significant value on it.

But in a few short years after business school graduation, you will become less "You (MBA-holder)," and more "You (What You Have Accomplished in Your Career)." Your academic credentials will matter much less than your category knowledge, functional expertise and demonstrated ability to get shit done. While the former should catalyze and improve upon the latter, it will be the latter that will determine your professional work progression.

Socially, the MBA will remain a pleasant calling card. It will serve as social short-hand to others that you are a smart, motivated person who was selected instead of nine other smart, motivated applicants for business school admission. So you get that little imprimatur.

This is all nice, but goes only so far. Once you're out for a few years, talking about your MBA is kind of like talking about what position you played in high school football. It makes you sound like a loser who lives in the past. (Btw, I played defensive tackle in high school…and I not only talk about my MBA, I've written a book about it. So what does that tell you?)

And while an MBA might help ignite your career as it did mine, you don't even need the degree to be successful.

Please indulge my last anecdote…

Having worked in the technology business for almost two decades, I have met several billionaires. I've done pretty well, but I am still a significant number of zeroes away from being one myself (though the massive profits from this book will surely close that gap).

Anyway, one day I was picking up my son from a play-date at one of these billionaires' houses (it's really nice). It was a mildly cold day so I was wearing my trusty old Dartmouth sweatshirt. I find it comfy because it's 20 years old and soft from hundreds of washings. I also find it comfy in a self-congratulatory, "I worked my ass off to get into and out of a great school and you should be impressed" kind of way.

Considering my very unfashionable attire, but with great sincerity, my friend asked, "Did you go to Dartmouth, Paul?"

Now's a good time to tell you that this self-made billionaire's highest degree is a BA from a large state university better known for its fraternities and football program than for its academic tradition.

"I did indeed," I answered her. "If you want, I can put in a good word for you with the admissions people. It would really give your career a boost."

In that moment of feeling like a boastful knucklehead, I was reminded clearly that what drives career success is not the degrees we compile or even our natural talents, but what we do with those gifts. Mark Zuckerberg and Bill Gates dropped out of college, for God's sake. I wonder if they ever break out their old Harvard sweatshirts, just to make themselves feel all warm inside.

My point here is that, while you may benefit from one immensely, the MBA itself ain't the goal.

An MBA is a tool, a weapon, an opportunity, a portal to help you discover yourself, be the best you and bring that best you to the business (or government or non-profit) world.

Business school is a gym where you build your strength and hone your strategy for the competition ahead. Having a fancy MBA may put you a rung or two up the ladder, but once you walk across that stage at graduation, the game starts all over again.

You may not retain many of the specific skills you learn in business school, just as muscles that aren't exercised will atrophy. Hell, I couldn't calculate the price of a bond today if you gave me Excel, a Goldman-Sachs intern and the price of the bond.

The stuff that matters, however, is (are?) the intangibles of the experience: the work ethic you will learn if you want to survive. The network you earn by bringing your best self to your classes, study groups and parties. The example of your brilliant classmates who will raise your standards of what you should expect from yourself.

If you do it right, what you achieve with your career and life won't come from any degree. It will come from your ambition, your resilience and your empathy. It will be the result of committing yourself to a path that challenges and excites you.

Remember—this whole thing is optional. You don't need an MBA to eat or breathe or procreate (though you very well might end up procreating with a business-school classmate).

So I—like the unrelenting admissions interviewer—will ask you once again: how will you use your MBA to power your career and life to achieve more than you would have without it?

Knowing that now will help you get the most out of the experience and the life that will be waiting for you on the other side.

Good luck. Enjoy the chicken wings.

Acknowledgements

After completing a 37,000 word book, knocking out 700 words of thanks should be a no-brainer. But completing this section has proven to be one of the most difficult parts of the whole project.

I am grateful to so many people and know almost exactly who they are, yet in earlier drafts of these acknowledgements I sailed right past gratitude toward sentimentality, then headlong into full-scale douchebaggery. I wrote garbage that fell just short of thanking "all the precious children of the world" and recognizing "fellow artists George Orwell, John Lennon and Jean-Michel Basquiat."

Please shoot me.

So I'm going to keep it simple and knock this last version out quick because I got kids to raise and more books to write.

I left my last corporate job a year and a half ago telling everyone that I was going to write a book. I had no idea what I was going to write about or how freaking hard it would be. If I knew then what I know now, I never would have started.

Somehow—thanks to equal parts hard work, persistence and naïveté—this book got done. I gave up several times, only to be pulled back on track by the encouragement of friends and family. I feel tremendous gratitude to all who helped me out overtly, covertly, explicitly or implicitly.

Let's start with the school folks.

Thank you to the faculty and staff of Dartmouth's Tuck School for a life-changing experience. To my Class of '97 classmates for inspiring me and making me laugh for two years in school and many years since. My life is much richer with you dorks in it.

Thank you to the Econ/Business faculty at Rhodes College for preparing me for this journey and to John Planchon and Paula

Jacobson who wrote my business school recommendations (thus proving that hyperbole can be an effective rhetorical tool).

To all the MBAs and business school students who completed the survey. I know it was a pain in the ass.

To those who read the various drafts of this book and provided feedback, candor and gentle redirection: Cole Ollinger, Rob Joseph, Steve Lubrano, Dan Lynch, Frank Hajdu, Vicki and Dave Craver (well Vicki anyway), Sander Biehn, Helen Kurtz, Zachary Brown, Patrick Ollinger, Merrick L. Furst, Ph.D., Jesse Itzler, Zach Obront, Mark Anten and Gigi Hadid.

To publishing industry editorly/writerly people who lent me their ear, expertise, guidance and connections: Jordan Pavlin, John Byrne, Peter Kafka, Peter Steiner, Gil Schwartz, Sean Beaudoin and Kendall Jenner.

To my painterly friend Brendan O'Connell for his advice, feedback and especially for giving me Steven Pressfield's *The War of Art*, the most important statements about work I have ever read. If you have a book, play or script burning inside of you, buy this book today. (Seriously, y'all.)

To editor / designer / book coach / all-around cool cat, Adam Robinson at Good Book Developers, for his steady hand, dry wit and good judgment.

To all the people who have been generous in their support and guidance in the recent or distant past: Josh Rahn, Andy Wiedlin, Jeff Berman, Dan Hart, Christien Louviere and especially Sandy and Martin Turbidy.

To Kiki Keating for working crazy hard to help get the word out. To my friend / personal writing trainer / co-conspirator, Jesse Dwyer. The next one is going to be even better.

To Al Bhatt for all kinds of stuff.

To Marshall Chiles and the team at the Laughing Skull Lounge in Atlanta and to Robert Hartmann, Dan Godfrey, Frank Kelley, Clark Douglas Clark and the staff of the Improvs in Brea, Irvine, and Ontario, CA for sharing their stages with me. I'm sorry you had to hear me tell the same jokes over and over. I've got lots of great new material working—I swear.

Finally, thank you to my children and to my wife Stacey for her love, support and Socratic guidance, which initially took the form of questions like "You're going to spend the next year writing a book about what?"

PHOTO: MIKE CARANO

PAUL OLLINGER IS A WRITER AND STAND-UP COMEDIAN who has opened for some of the biggest names in the business. He also has an MBA from Dartmouth's Tuck School and was one the first 250 employees of Facebook, where he served as VP of Sales for the Western United States. When he's not on the road speaking, doing stand-up and sharing his unique POV on business and life, he is playing golf, binge watching *Charlie Rose* or checking Who's Viewed Your Profile on LinkedIn. He lives in Atlanta, GA with his beautiful wife, two wonderful children and French bulldog, Colonel Tom Parker.